HARD TRUTH

TODD CARNEY

with TONY ADAMS

HARD TRUTH

ALLEN&UNWIN
SYDNEY • MELBOURNE • AUCKLAND • LONDON

Every effort has been made to trace the holders of copyright material. If you have any information concerning copyright material in this book please contact the publishers at the address below.

Grateful acknowledgement is given for permission to reprint 'NRL's double standards slammed over Matt Lodge and Todd Carney situations' from *Sporting News*, 2 March 2018.

Allen & Unwin
83 Alexander Street
Crows Nest NSW 2065
Australia
Phone: (61 2) 8425 0100
Email: info@allenandunwin.com
Web: www.allenandunwin.com

A catalogue record for this book is available from the National Library of Australia

ISBN 978 1 76087 603 6

Internal design by Simon Paterson, Bookhouse, Sydney
Set in 12.7/19.9 pt Simoncini Garamond Std by Bookhouse, Sydney
Printed and bound in Australia by Griffin Press, part of Ovato

10 9 8 7 6 5 4 3 2 1

The paper in this book is FSC® certified. FSC® promotes environmentally responsible, socially beneficial and economically viable management of the world's forests.

To my parents—my late dad Daryl and my best mate, my mum Leanne—your dedication and encouragement helped me realise my dreams and your unconditional love got me through the tough times.

CONTENTS

PROLOGUE

One of my favourite Aussie songs is Redgum's 'I Was Only 19', and for some reason I found myself nervously humming it in the middle of the 2004 season sitting on the reserves bench at Central Coast Stadium. I was two years younger than the hero of the song, who was fighting in the Vietnam War, and I have always admired the courage of our soldiers who show such bravery so we can enjoy our freedom.

In no way am I comparing myself to the soldier, or war to football, but I was about to fight my own battle—my NRL debut against big Willie Mason and the Bulldogs, 'the Dogs of War' as they liked to call themselves, because of their fierce reputation on the field. Only a few months earlier I was happily watching Willie and his mates on TV at home in Goulburn—now I was about to face them head on . . . I could barely believe it. I kept looking down at my lime green Canberra jersey and pinching myself. This was the high point of my life, finally making first grade, and doing it while still a raw teenager fresh out of school.

It was extra special because I was playing in front of my mum and dad, who sacrificed so much to get me to that point of my life, as well as all my friends and family. Mum and Dad spent countless hours driving me all around the state as a kid, to schoolboy carnivals, representative games and the like—all to make this moment possible. It took a huge chunk out of their lives, innumerable weekends lost to motoring all over the country when they could have been home enjoying life.

This was the night I was going to repay them for their sacrifice and dedication, and hopefully make my friends and family proud as well. They had all made the trip to Gosford to watch me make my debut. The nerves got edgier and edgier as the game went on—I knew my moment of truth was drawing closer. Maybe I had arrived. Maybe I would go out there and not be up to it, and never be seen in first grade again. Career over at seventeen. It's happened to plenty of players—would I join the list? I knew I would get my chance out in the middle at some stage in the second half and that little voice inside my head kept telling me, 'Just don't make a fool of yourself out there, Todd.'

Finally, a trainer relayed the message from our coach Matty Elliott: 'Carney, you're on—get out there,' and my legs almost went to jelly. I walked to the sideline and Willie looked at me and smiled, like a dog sizing up a juicy bone. He was even bigger and meaner than I imagined. He made sure I just about threw up my lunch when he smiled and growled, 'Come on, young pup—I've been waiting for this all day.'

I'd been a Canberra fan since I was a little kid, and to run onto the field with the likes of Simon Woolford, Clinton Schifcofske, Mark McLinden and Ruben Wiki was a dream come true. How many people get to live out their wildest dreams? Not many, I bet, and I felt incredibly lucky—and still do every time I think back to that amazing day. Mix that with nerves and excitement, and I was totally over-whelmed as I ran onto the field.

For the first few minutes, I was like a deer in the head-lights. The hits were so hard, the pace of the game so fast. I felt lost and alone, like a spectator dragged from the stands into the middle of this carnage. But my teammates gave me a few words of encouragement and I did some good things with the ball.

After the first few touches, I calmed down and got to work, doing what I had trained for since the age of four.

It was all I ever wanted to do, and this was the start of my journey. The Bulldogs were a team of stars—a few months later they would win the grand final—but we pushed them all the way to the end. They were ahead 24–20 when we launched a late surge. As the siren sounded, we were on the attack and a try was 'on', but their renowned defence shut us down.

The boys were shattered and of course I would have loved to win, but I was still feeling elated. I had come through unscathed and shown I wasn't out of my depth. I knew I would only get better. After this taste, I wanted more, and I was on track to become a real rugby league player.

•

Fast forward three years and I had the world at my feet. I was a regular first-grader, making good money and playing great football—I was living my dream. But the demon drink, which so often brought me undone, was about to hit me big time.

I'd just bought my first apartment in Bruce in Canberra, and the tiler called me to tell me he'd finished his work and the place was ready to go. I'd had a few beers but was so excited to see the place I talked my teammate Steve Irwin into letting me drive his ute.

We were almost there—it was only a short drive—when I rounded a corner and spun the wheels. Next thing I saw the dreaded flashing blue lights behind me. I didn't have a driver's licence at the time and already had a bit of a reputation around town with the cops and the media.

I panicked. Instead of pulling over, which I've wished I did 1000 times since, I hit the accelerator and did a runner. I knew all the back streets and thought I could lose the cops. *Stupid.* It was the classic 'fight-or-flight' response in the heat of the moment and, before long, we were cornered in a cul-de-sac.

Steve had a knee injury and wasn't going anywhere. Me, I opened the door and ran for it like a mad fool. It was dark and the cops were on my tail with flashlights. I saw a big tree in a quiet street—and started climbing. I had some coins in my pocket and threw them away so they wouldn't rattle. My childhood on the farm proved handy—I went up the tree like a monkey and was ten metres off the ground as the cops circled beneath me, scratching their heads. They were looking left, right, straight ahead and behind them, but luckily not *up*. I found out later that they would have brought the dogs out to find me, but there was a music festival on nearby.

I was barefoot, the wind was blowing and it was freezing, but the adrenaline was kicking in and I wasn't going anywhere. I called my manager and told him what

I had just done. He said, 'Where are you now?' When I told him I was up in a tree he just laughed. That broke the tension a little . . . but only for a few seconds. I decided to go home to Goulburn, back to my parents, and work out my next move.

It seems funny now, but sitting in that tree I was shaking with fear and shame. I had already put my poor parents through all sorts of heartache, but this was by far the worst thing I had done. I had slipped up by making yet another poor decision on the drink—not for the first time and, sadly, far from the last.

•

How can a career contain this many ups and downs? How have I managed to go from triumph to disaster, all of my own doing? These are questions I ask myself all the time. Having written the story of my life, I'm still not sure I'm closer to an answer, but it's a pretty good tale.

1

A BUSH LAD

Growing up in a country town like Goulburn was fun, even though there wasn't an awful lot for a kid to do there back in the late 1980s and early 1990s, compared to these days— no iPads or internet and the like—not that it bothered me. I was born there in 1986, and it was a nice place to live, despite the freezing cold winters and sweltering summers of the Southern Tablelands of New South Wales. There were three of us kids—my eldest sister Krysten, my other sister Melinda and me, the 'baby' of the family. My parents Leanne and Daryl were great to us. I was picked on a little by my sisters, being the youngest, but protected by them at the same time.

Mum says I was a bit of a loner in my early years, happy to play in the backyard by myself with what few toys I had. My life became a lot more interesting when I was eight and we left town and moved out onto the land. It was always my dad's dream to have a farm and we settled on a property called Boxer's Creek. There were horses, cows and other animals. Dad was over the moon and I loved it too, it was much more fun for a little kid than living in town. I spent plenty of time with my dad, and if I wasn't learning off him about country life, I was with my Pop, Lindsay. It was a happy time. Pop, my dad's dad, was a real country man as well. He'd be there at 6 o'clock every morning just pottering around and I enjoyed hanging out helping him and Dad with chores on the farm. I spent many hours in Dad's truck or Pop's truck, driving around the property or into town, talking and learning and asking a thousand questions, as young kids do.

I'd get into little bits of mischief every so often, not uncommon for kids that age, but I wasn't too bad. Pop had a few grandkids but I like to think I was his favourite. In school holidays we would often go fishing, just the two of us, and they are special memories. I've got mates around the world through football, but family has always been special to me. Growing up, we were all very close and I remain very tight with Mum and my sisters. I believe without family you are nothing, and my family helped me make it to the top in football—no way could I have made it without their help and support. Dad and Pop have both passed now and I often wonder how my life would be if they were still around, but it is one of those things I'll never know—all I know is that I loved them and miss them. As for Mum, I have always thought of her as my best friend and still do. We have a special bond. As the youngest she spoilt me, but at the same time, she always gave me plenty of chores to do—probably to keep me out of strife! We never went without anything, so we were lucky. My sisters were big on sport: my middle sister Melinda played netball at a high level and loved the competition. Krysten also played plenty of sport and was a bit of an allrounder. I loved running around and tried my hand at just about every sport available in the bush in the 1990s. Touch football, cricket, basketball—I loved them all. About the only sports I didn't play were rugby union and soccer, which held no interest for me. Rugby league quickly became number one.

I started at age four, playing under 6s for North Goulburn—and I hated it! I didn't like it one bit, and felt like I had been thrown into the great unknown. I was little, and I worried I would get bashed around and picked on out there. I was always pretty shy and still am, to some extent, in new surroundings. I don't like being the centre of attention. We'd arrive at games and I wouldn't want to get out of the car, let alone play. But Mum was smart—she'd pay me a $5 bribe with the promise of a can of Coke and lollies after the game, and off I went to join my mates on the field—that's all it took. I often wonder where I would be now if I hadn't taken the bribes!

It was hard. The other kids were older and bigger than me and most were mates at kindergarten. I hadn't started school yet and felt very much the outsider. I started school early at age four-and-a-half at Wollondilly Public School in Goulburn, but repeated Year 1. Mum thought I was too young for my age and she wanted me to have a bit more time to grow up and learn things properly. I wasn't real happy at the time but, in hindsight, it was probably a good thing for me. I ended up in my right age group and made good mates. I wasn't the smartest kid at school, that's for sure. But having said that, I don't think I was the dumbest kid either. I was sort of middle of the road and just went about my business, like other kids trying to find their way.

On the football field, I wasn't a standout player at primary school, in my opinion, although someone must have thought otherwise because I made the NSW Primary Schools Sports Association regional team. Twins Brett and Josh Morris were also in the side and we became good mates and are still friends to this day. We also played together for South Coast Schoolboys for several years from under 11s and it was great to reunite with them at State of Origin for New South Wales more than a decade later. I'd often visit them in Kiama in the school holidays and we also spent plenty of time together when we played for New South Wales in junior footy.

At around age eleven I switched clubs to Goulburn Stockmen and we had a pretty good side—I don't think we lost a game from under 11s to under 16s. We played in the Canberra comps and I remember one game in particular in the final of the 'Blocker' Roach Cup. It was the two best under 11 teams in the state and we met Cambridge Park, who went in as raging hot favourites. Even though I was the playmaker, I never felt pressure to win those big games—except from Dad. He was pumped all week and made sure I was 'up' for the match. I went okay and we beat Cambridge Park, which was big news in Goulburn at the time. I made plenty of rep sides during my school days but never made the Australian Schoolboys, which is a bit of a regret. But you have to remember there were some bloody good halfbacks around throughout my career, and I thought I was fortunate to play representative football at all. Even though the Raiders promised I would do Year

11 and Year 12 in Canberra once they signed me, it never happened, and that made it virtually impossible for me to play Australian Schoolboys.

I made the Canberra junior rep sides and had some success. In 2005 Parramatta were undefeated all year and we met them in the final of the S.G. Ball Cup. They were unbackable favourites but we put it all together on the day. I did okay, and we knocked them off in the big one, which was an amazing feeling. It was only the second time the Raiders had won the title and the club treated us like conquering heroes—we loved it.

•

As far as footy was concerned, Dad was a perfectionist and probably a bit hard on me. He was a tough taskmaster and stayed that way right until he started to get sick. He taught me a lot about rugby league and life in general. Dad knew a fair bit about footy and also coached me and my mates. In his heyday, they tell me he was a pretty fair player for Goulburn United—a halfback of course, like me. He was highly regarded in bush footy circles and old Don Furner, the first coach of the Raiders in the early 1980s, had a high opinion of him. Dad was never interested in playing in Sydney but bush footy was strong back then and they got good crowds. After two daughters, he was delighted to have a son and never made any secret of the fact that he wanted me to follow in his footsteps and be a rugby league player.

Of course Dad took a special interest in me and my development on the field. He wanted me to be a good player right from the start and success came fairly easy to me, which I owe to him. He saw I had talent and wanted me to be the best I could be. Not just on the footy field, but at training, on the cricket pitch and the like. Pop could see Dad was pushing me, and he was a bit protective of me as a result. I guess Pop thought for a kid, football should be fun and he wanted me to enjoy myself. If I played well, I got praise from Dad, but if I had a bad game, I'd be in the doghouse. Some days if I had a poor game I'd sit in the back seat of the car and Dad wouldn't say a word to me all the way from Sydney back to Goulburn. It felt like the drive took days. When we went on a holiday to, say, the Gold Coast, we'd go to a theme park in the morning like Wet'n'Wild and then in the afternoon Dad would say, 'Come on, let's go,' and we'd head to the nearest park to do skills and fitness training. When we went to the shops, it wasn't to hunt for souvenirs or comfort food, it was to buy protein powder and stuff like that.

I remember one day I had three mates from my team around and Dad said, 'Come on, boys, let's go for a drive.'

We were silly kids, probably around eleven, and didn't ask any questions. I remember seeing four rusty old pushbikes in the back of Dad's ute but again, didn't think anything of it. So Dad drove us around 30 kilometres from home and stopped the ute in the middle of nowhere and said, 'Right, everybody out!' Then he took the four pushbikes from the back of the ute, making sure I had the hardest one to pedal, of course. Then he said to us, 'Alright—ride these back home.' Our jaws dropped, but we did as we were told. He rode behind us in the ute the whole way just to make sure we didn't get up to any funny business, while our dog ran alongside us. I felt sorry for the poor mutt—he was rooted by the time we got home. We rode for what felt like forever. It was dark when we got back, exhausted, but it was great for our fitness and, as young kids, we were active and happy to take on the challenge, even though I felt like stopping a few times.

During footy games, I always had to take note of where Dad was sitting and look to him for hand signals during breaks in play. He'd usually give me a thumbs up when I was going well . . . but I dreaded it when he gave me the thumbs down. Mum once asked me, 'Are you going to be as hard as he was on you when you have kids?' I thought long and hard before answering. In the end, I told her, 'Probably, yes . . . I think so. I wouldn't force them to play rugby league but if they did, I would do all I could to help them realise their potential and be the best player they could be.'

Dad was hard and it wasn't always fun, but I knew he had my best interests at heart, even though there were times I wished he would back off and just let me be a normal kid like my mates. Pop saw the negative effect that the pressure from Dad sometimes had on me—constantly having to be the best—and the two of them clashed a bit over that. It got to the stage where the pressure became too much and at around age twelve I decided to 'retire'. It all got too hard. I wanted a normal childhood. I wasn't allowed to ride skateboards and there was no partying because I had to look after my body. I resented it a bit, seeing all my mates have fun like kids are supposed to, and rebelled against Dad's tough approach. Pop was on my side and said to me, 'You're entitled to push him away.' I appreciated his support.

My retirement lasted all of one week and, looking back, it was probably nothing more than a hissy-fit from a kid who didn't like to be pushed too hard. But at the same time, I think it sent Dad a message that I was still just a little kid and wanted to enjoy my footy more than anything else.

I probably only realised I had true potential when I started at Mulwaree High School, Goulburn. I came to see that I could make things happen on the field. It felt special to be good at something and be appreciated for it.

I started training with the Goulburn Stockmen one or two nights a week and all of a sudden the Canberra Raiders began to take notice of me. I was chosen to join their junior development squad and Dad or one of the other parents would drive me to Canberra for training up to three nights a week. Dad was the coach of the Stockmen team the year below me. He really knew how things worked and put a lot of time and effort into developing my game.

In late high school, my confidence grew and, training with Canberra, I developed a dream to play in the NRL. I put all my time, focus and effort into the dream and stopped caring about schoolwork. I had a goal and wasn't about to let things like maths and science take my mind off it. Mum and Dad supported me—they could see football was where my future lay and they didn't give me a hard time about my grades. I don't think some teachers were very happy about my career path but, having said that, I also wasn't a bad kid. I stayed out of trouble at school and I think I can thank footy for that, it was on my mind 24/7. I was too scared to play up: no wagging school or getting suspended. I knew I would have been in strife when I got home and it also might have affected my football prospects.

I finished Year 10 and took a scholarship with the Raiders. I was meant to go to Erindale College in Canberra for Years 11 and 12—a fancy school that Ricky Stuart and lots of other good players went to. On reflection, it might have been a better thing for me.

MUM

If they handed out medals to long-suffering mothers, Leanne Carney must surely be a five-star general by now. The mum of Todd Carney has been to hell and back with her son—as well as fighting her own personal battles—but has always stood by her youngest child. A down-to-earth, chatty character, Leanne works as a nurse.

'I'm a Goulburn girl, born and raised,' she says proudly. 'I met Todd's dad Daryl when I was around eighteen. He was a good local footy player and I'd go watch him play. Daryl was desperate for a boy to follow in his footsteps. Our first two kids were girls and I reckon he would have kept having kids with me until we had a boy. Fortunately, number three came out and the doctor said to us, "I think we have a little half-back here." If only he knew how prophetic his words would be! Then we had Todd circumcised and the doctor said, "Now he's a quarterback!"'

But father and son were very different in temperament, Leanne was to observe as her son grew and began playing competitive sport. 'Daryl was much more fiery than Todd. He had an offer to play in Sydney but knocked it back—he was a bush lad,' Leanne says. 'He loved to fight on the field and back in those days, that was just a part of the game—you traded a few punches when the game started, got it out of your system and got on with the game. How different it is now. But Daryl also liked a pub stoush and, again, back then they were just a part of country life. He got a bit of a reputation around town and anyone who wanted a fight, Daryl would accommodate them. Todd has never thrown a punch on the field in his life, I don't think. He is an easy-going kid and just loves playing the game . . . he's a lover, not a fighter,' she laughs.

Leanne recalls the problem she had convincing her baby boy to play rugby league in his early days. 'He was the smallest kid on sign-up day and he was terrified,' she says. 'He would hide between my legs and beg, "Mum, *please* don't make me play." But we thought it would be good for him and teach him some discipline and, once he got out there, he was fine. His father was hard on him, but only because Daryl could see the potential and talent there. One weekend Daryl went away on a work trip and Todd said to me, "I'm not playing today." I knew we would both be in trouble if Daryl came home and Todd hadn't put on the boots, so I promised him $5 if he went out and scored a try. So the little bugger agreed . . . and went out and scored *five* tries. I had to hand over $25—I wasn't happy!

'Todd hated school with a similar passion. When he started school, he was younger than most of the kids at four-and-a-half and would rip his uniform off hoping that would get him a day off. But, like with the footy, he slowly settled into it and after a couple of years, he went from shy little kid to Dennis the Menace. Nothing major, but he loved throwing stones or anything he could get his hands on and he couldn't sit still—he loved being active. I remember one day I arrived at school to pick him up and the teacher had him out front. I thought "Oh no, what's he done now?" She explained it was no major drama, but he was tackling all the kids in class . . . and she said it was a non-contact school! So I had to try to explain to him to keep his tackling for the football field. Todd was also a good cricketer but tore his groin a few times. Eventually he had to decide between the two sports and with his dad having an input, it was an easy call—the pads were put away and it was footy, footy and footy.'

The youngster quickly developed a name in Goulburn footy and became a target. 'One game, Todd was blitzing them so a kid on the other team punched him in the head—it was blatant and a cheap shot,' Leanne says. 'His two sisters are much more fiery than him—more like his dad—and they yelled out "Punch him back, Todd." But that just wasn't the type of kid Todd was. We told him he should never fight but I don't think we needed to—he was always a gentle, caring kid. When that other kid punched him, he just got up, collected himself, and got on with the game.'

Leanne admits that her husband was a bit hard on the budding star. 'There were no sleepovers the night before a game, no riding skateboards in case he fell and broke an arm or a leg. He was pretty strict,' she says. 'It got on Todd's nerves. All his friends could be normal kids and he was training like a professional footballer at twelve. One day Todd hurt his ankle playing but his dad insisted "You'll be right." The next day we went to watch the Raiders play in Canberra and Daryl told Todd to play footy on the hill with the other kids, even though the ankle was still sore. So he did. The next morning, I went to wake him for school and his ankle was swollen like a balloon. I could make out the outline of it under the sheets. Of course it was broken. I made Daryl take him straight to hospital. But even that didn't stop Todd—he had to have the plaster around the ankle replaced three times because he was so active, he wore through it!

'Daryl's dad Lindsay was more moderate and sometimes I'd have to call Lindsay up and tell him, "Your son is being too hard on the boy. Can you get him to ease up?" He would come over and defuse the situation and tell Daryl to pull his head in. Looking back, I think that was part of Todd's problems. He couldn't enjoy a normal childhood when he was young and so he lived out his childhood in his mid-twenties—and you can't do that these days, especially when you are a big-name footy star and everyone is watching your every move, ready to put it on social media and TV and the back page of the newspaper.'

THE SISTERS

Todd is extremely close to his two older sisters, Krysten and Melinda, but that hasn't stopped the two girls tipping the bucket on the troubled star, albeit in a light-hearted and loving way. The duo reveal that, among a host of other childhood misdemeanours, Carney had his first ride in a police car when he was just five years old.

'Todd has been in a few paddy wagons in his time, but not many people know he was barely out of nappies when he had his first [ride],' Krysten says. 'He was set to go for a sleep-over at our Auntie Robyn's house and was all excited before the event. But once he got there, it was all too much for him, because he was such a shy kid. He broke down and started crying and so Robyn packed him up with all his sleeping gear in her car and started to drive him back to our family home in Goulburn. But she broke down and was stranded on the side of the road. Luckily, a paddy wagon was driving past and took pity on them and gave them a ride. I think Todd was all excited—he said they flashed the blue lights for him. Maybe that's where his like of paddy wagons started!'

The family was a little surprised when the paddy wagon pulled up at their modest Goulburn brick home but not at Todd's antics. 'When it came to sleeping over at people's houses, Todd would be all for it and wanting to go until it came time to go to bed,' Krysten says. 'Then he would throw a tantrum and cry like a baby until Mum or Dad went to pick him up, he just didn't feel comfortable. After a while most of his friends used to come to our house for sleepovers. He was a mummy's boy and still is!' she laughs. 'He was always a bit sooky as a kid and liked cuddles, especially from Mum, and she would always gladly oblige. They had a special bond—and still do actually.'

Mum Leanne spoilt her only son, balancing out the some-times harsh treatment of dad Daryl, who pushed the youngster to the limit to make him the great player he became. 'He was the youngest of the three of us and the only boy so yeah, he got special treatment, but we didn't mind,' Melinda says. 'Mum and Dad supported all three of us in everything we did so there was never any jealousy or anything like that. We were all very close and went to each other's sporting events and cheered each other on. We never missed out on anything and had some wonderful family holidays as kids at places like the Gold Coast, NSW South Coast and the Whitsundays.'

The girls had no doubt where Todd's future lay, even when he was barely old enough to read. 'He grew up in the era when Tina Turner sang "Simply the Best" and it became the game's anthem,' Krysten remembers. 'He could watch that ad on TV all day long—he just loved it. We have a video of him sitting in the bubble bath, singing like Tina, and by then he'd seen it so many times he knew all the words. After that, he would sing the Canberra Raiders' "Bad and mean, the Green Machine" song—he knew that one word-for-word too. And he told anyone who would listen that when he was big, he would one day play for the Raiders. His Raiders jumper was his favourite shirt—he wore it everywhere.

'But footy wasn't his only interest. While he learned to be hard on the football field and show no pain, he was a softy at heart. He has always loved emotional movies and when we all watched *Free Willy* together, he would cry—even the tenth time we saw it. We made fun of him and he would run and hide behind the curtain so we couldn't see him, or he'd pretend he had something in his eye that was making it tear up—but we knew better. He was the sweetest kid. On cold winter nights he would snuggle next to any one of us by the heater, and even now when he comes home, he's been known to do the same. He may have been through some tough times and be a bad boy in the eyes of those that don't know him, but at the end of the day he is still a big kid at heart and he is our Toddy—and we love him unconditionally.'

The young Todd had a good throwing arm, which he used to good effect in cricket but also led to drama more than once. 'He became obsessed with throwing rocks—not in a bad way— he loved throwing them at lakes or in the woods,' Krysten says. 'But he broke more than one window with mistimed throws.

He also liked to stand on the road and try to throw his rocks onto the backs of trucks that were zooming past . . . until Dad found out and explained that that was a "no-no".

'When we lived on the farm, he and Melinda went exploring one day and ended up in a neighbour's backyard. For some reason our chooks weren't laying eggs, but their chooks were laying plenty. So Todd and Mel "borrowed" a bunch of their eggs and ran home with their booty. Again, it was left to Mum and Dad to straighten things out and they marched the two of them back down to the neighbours and made them return the eggs and apologise—and promise never to steal anything again. If the media had got hold of that, it probably would have made the back page!

'Trouble did seem to follow Todd from an early age, even when he didn't mean any harm. Once we were on holidays in Gerroa and Todd got a new fishing line—he always loved to fish, especially with his grandfather. He was casting the line, getting the feel of it, off a bridge above the road. But he accidentally hit a flashy car with his rod and sinker and the driver wasn't impressed. He screeched to a halt and chased Todd all the way back to the caravan park where we were staying. Luckily for Todd, he was fast from an early age and got home before the bloke caught up with him—but the guy did have a few stern words with Mum and Dad. Then one birthday our parents made a bit of a tactical error by buying Todd a pellet gun. He wasn't allowed skateboards or anything else that could end up injuring him for football, so the slug gun was kind of a compromise. Todd set up a bunch of little plastic characters he had collected from McDonald's Happy Meals in a line and was shooting at them one by one. But being a young kid, he didn't think of what could go wrong and after a few minutes a neighbour who was out going for a leisurely stroll had a pellet go whistling past his ear.

'Todd had a very sheltered teenage life—no parties, no drinking, no hanging around downtown—he gave up a lot under Dad's watchful eye to become a star. Dad even had him on a strict curfew, which occasionally we broke. Dad would get mad, but [me and Mel] said it was our fault so he wouldn't get in too much trouble.'

When he wasn't upsetting the neighbours, football domin-ated the young Todd's life. 'We lived on a big farm and it was a great place for kids to grow up and explore,' Melinda says. 'We had horses, cows and sheep in the paddock—as well as a set of goalposts made by Dad so Todd could practise his goal kicking. Football pretty much was our lives. Dad was a good judge and he could tell we had a special talent in our midst. Dad pushed Todd hard, but it did bring out the best in him, even though he sometimes didn't like the pressure. Dad was the team coach and Mum was the manager and we spent most weekends travelling all over the state to carnivals and matches. Todd was usually the smallest kid on the field in the juniors but he was also the best. He was so fast the opposition couldn't catch him and we would cheer him all the way to the tryline. As he grew up and became a star, we kept up the family tradition, going to as many matches as we could to cheer him on, even when he was up in Atherton in Queensland, Byron Bay and in Europe. Both of us girls are married now with kids and they love Todd—they come with us to games and are always decked out in the gear of whatever team he is playing for at the time. We remain very close and when we can't get to games, we are always sending him messages saying "good luck", just so he knows we are thinking of him. We are his number one supporters but also his biggest critics, and we are proud of what he has achieved and the person he has grown to become.'

2

THE GREEN MACHINE

In 2003, Matty Elliott was the Canberra Raiders coach and he called me into his office one day. He asked me if I enjoyed school and why I was planning on doing Years 11 and 12 in Canberra. I told him school wasn't really my thing and that I was just going there for the football program. So he asked if I wanted to train with the Canberra squad full-time. I was floating on cloud nine—it was a huge step towards realising my goal. For me and Dad, it was a dream come true.

Mum wasn't so sure. She knew how young I was in terms of maturity—I was still only sixteen—and thought it would have been best for my development to finish school and get more experience of the world in those final two years at Erindale College. She also realised I would be hanging out with grown men, not my mates the same age as me, and she had some serious reservations about that. Mum and Dad had a few heavy discussions about it, but whatever she said pretty much fell on deaf ears with Dad. I can see now that Mum had a good point and my best interests at heart. I should probably have done those last two years at school, matured a bit and got a trade I could use after footy. But Dad had put so much time and effort into getting me to this stage he didn't want to risk letting such an amazing opportunity go—and neither did I.

The chance to join a full-time NRL squad was a massive step, especially at the club I had supported since I was three years old. Dad and I both wanted it so badly—no way were we going to let a little thing like school get in the way. I explained to Matty that all I really wanted to do was play rugby league, and I am forever grateful that he gave me a crack at it.

I joined the Raiders in 2003 at seventeen and it was surreal. Suddenly I was playing and training alongside guys I worshipped, most I had only seen on TV. Guys like Ruben Wiki, Jason Croker, Luke Davico, Mark McLinden and Simon Woolford were Canberra legends and to me it was an honour just to be training on the same paddock as them. My first day, I remember I sidled up alongside 'Toots' Croker. He grew up in Crookwell near me at Goulburn and we were old family friends—I knew he would look after me. For the first few weeks, I think I followed him around like a little lost puppy—he probably got sick of the sight of me. I was like a small kid and part of me felt that I didn't deserve to be there, that they were all better than me, which at that stage they probably were, especially in terms of football toughness and definitely experience.

It all came too quickly. I went from being a schoolkid watching Andrew Johns on TV and idolising him, to playing against him a couple of years later. I was so shy I wouldn't take my shorts off in the showers and that caused a lot of gee-ups and funny comments from the boys. When I became a senior player, I came across other young blokes who felt the same and I'd make the same funny cracks that were directed at me. It's the cycle of life I guess.

I was always doing my hair before games and training. I wanted to look good but it was also a by-product of having a sister, Melinda, who is a hairdresser. The boys used to give me a hard time over that. I turned up at training with weird and wonderful hairstyles more than once: blond streaks, even dashes of pink—courtesy of Melinda—and the older boys loved giving me grief. I didn't mind. Melinda used me as her guinea pig a few times when it came to trying out new cuts, and they weren't always a success!

Matty was a good reader of minds and I think he sensed that lack of confidence I had in myself. He was forever telling me that I was there on my merits and would repay his faith in me. So I knuckled down, trained hard and did the best I could. It's not easy at seventeen training and playing against grown men—it was like when I was four playing against six-year-olds all over again. Tough mentally and physically, and quite intimidating. But I was determined to make a go of it, now I had come this far, and I hit the gym. I put on a heap of weight that first year in a bid to make myself stronger and tougher.

In the end, I put on a bit too much weight and struggled with the running side of my game. Our trainer, Carl Jennings, got me in at 6 a.m. every morning to strip some of the weight back off me. I lived at the Australian Institute of Sport and trained with the elite academy squad. I felt very lucky indeed. A few of the other young guys in the squad lived there too and we had some good times after training, hanging out and enjoying the Canberra nightlife. But deep down, I missed Goulburn and family and I would sneak home, which was less than an hour away, most nights after training, just because I felt more comfortable there.

•

In the trials, I must have done okay because I expected to start in the under 20s but I skipped that. I was fast-tracked and selected straight into reserve grade, which was coached by former Raiders hooker Wayne Collins.

In my junior footy, I wasn't a big talker or organiser; instead I relied on my individual talent to get me through. But now things were different—this was reserve grade and I was playing in the team that won the grand final the year before. So it was a big step up from under 17s in just a few months—and the heat was on. At training, Wayne brought in a rule that I was the only person on the field allowed to speak. It was awkward at first but there was a method to his madness—I soon started talking, just to break the silence, and it became a part of my game.

My reserve grade form earned me a call-up to the first team: here was my chance to play NRL football. After a few games on the bench, I finally got to make my debut against the Bulldogs and can remember being a bundle of nerves in the build-up. My dream was about to become reality, but it was pretty terrifying. Confidence was not high on my list of qualities as a teenager and there were plenty of self-doubts.

Matty called me into his office one day—I had no idea why—and told me my time had come to play first grade. He said he wasn't sure where he would play me or when I would come off the bench, a lot would depend on the situation in the match and how things panned out. It was a moment I'll never forget. I hadn't really been happy in Canberra up until that point but this made it all so worth it, and I could finally see the purpose of being there.

Calling Mum and Dad and telling them I was about to play NRL football remains one of the sweetest moments of my life. Aged seventeen, I became the fourth youngest player to debut for the Raiders—behind Laurie Daley, Todd Payten and Brett Finch—and that knowledge only added to my nerves. 'The plan wasn't to let Todd play first grade so early, but his form simply demanded it,' Matty said to the media, who all grilled him about why he chose me.

I was shitting myself leading up to the actual game, which was at Central Coast Stadium, mid-season in Round 15. The Bulldogs always prided themselves on their tough pack—'the Dogs of War'. Willie Mason was in his prime then and I knew he loved to give it to young blokes and test them out. He was about three times the size of me and ran like a freight train. In the nights leading up to the game I had a few nightmares about trying to bring Mason down and him trampling me with those massive boots. Willie also loved to sledge and I was certain he would have a crack or two at me, although by 2004 sledging had gone out of the game to a large extent. The game was so fast, you didn't have time to sledge blokes in most instances. When I finally came on I looked up and, sure enough, there was Willie, with a big smile on his face, looking straight at me with those big piercing eyes. I just about shat myself then and there. He tested me out a few times—I just hung on to a leg for dear life as he charged at me, and luckily a couple of teammates helped me bring him to a halt.

I've got to know Willie in recent years and he is a great fella—and he was a real personality in an era when there were few personalities in the game—and we laugh about that afternoon up in Gosford. Sadly, it was Willie who got the last laugh. It was a close game and we could have won it with some late chances but the Bulldogs edged us out. A few months later, they went on to win the comp, beating the Roosters in the grand final, so it was a fair effort from our boys.

We snuck into the finals in eighth spot, but met the Roosters—who were favourites to win the trophy—in the opening weekend of the finals and they beat us easily. I watched from the bench. Matty didn't think I was ready for the intensity of finals football and he was right. It was a level above the week-to-week club stuff and the plan was always to blood me slowly—I had no complaints about not being out there. In that first season, Matty dropped me quite a few times, just to keep me grounded and fresh. When he did drop me, I struggled a bit in reserve grade. I'm not sure if it was a mental thing or whatever, but I realised this was one area of my game I had to pick up: you have to mentally and physically perform every weekend, irrespective of where you are playing.

•

I turned eighteen in June and the club must have liked what they saw in me because they gave me a four-year deal mid-season after just two NRL games—the first time they have ever done that for an eighteen-year-old. Matty was the driving force behind the long deal. He really believed in me and I didn't want to let him down. 'I have so much respect for Todd and our recruitment in the halves has been based around him,' Elliott told the media when my new deal was announced. 'It's not something we would normally do with a young player—sign them for such a long period—but Todd's talent really demanded we did.'

There was a lot of hype around me, and also Josh Dugan, who came through the next year. People saw it as the start of an exciting new era for Canberra and neither one of us handled it real well, looking back. We were just kids who liked having a good time suddenly thrust into the limelight and the pressure. Unless that has happened to you, it is hard to describe the burden that it suddenly creates, and how hard it is to handle. There were many times I wished I was just an average guy with an average job who could go out and have fun with his mates without the whole world watching and waiting to pounce—and I know plenty of other players who feel the same. Yes, we are blessed to get good money to play the game we love, but it's not the perfect life some like to make it out to be.

I was lucky enough to play for NSW Residents that first year and also played NSW under 19s. It was a huge thing for me to get recognised by the representative selectors in my first season of senior footy. We went okay against our Queensland counterparts, winning 20–12 in the curtain raiser to State of Origin game one at Telstra Stadium. The next year, Matty rewarded me for my good pre-season form by throwing me in with the first-grade team for a trial against the Bulldogs. I played in the centres for some reason and the opposition were a real handful once they worked up a head of steam. I didn't do anything great that day, but I also didn't let them get around me too often, and that early taste gave me a lot of confidence.

Matty always had faith in me and I regard him as one of the best coaches I had in my career. He was different—he cared about you as a person and not just as a footballer. He also brought in a lot of innovations that worked well at the Raiders, and we overachieved in the time he was there, making the finals more than once.

Matty saw potential in me and that was what a shy kid from the bush needed. When he moved on to Penrith, I almost followed him. Ditto the Warriors when he went there—that's how highly I rated him. We still talk regularly and I bounce ideas off him. He is always there for me and a genuine mate who thinks outside the square.

•

The 2005 season came along and things had changed again. I'd gone from a kid no one really knew who had played a handful of top-grade games, to a more regular member of the team who opponents and rival coaches were starting to take note of. Pace was definitely my strength at that stage. Matty told me at the start of the year that he wouldn't throw me back in the deep end in first grade from Round 1, but would put me in and out of the team to allow me to get used to the pace of the NRL and make it a smoother transition. While I wasn't all that thrilled about this, it showed me that he cared about my development and wanted me to be a long-term first-grade player once I earned my stripes.

MATTHEW ELLIOTT

Matthew Elliott still remembers the day in the early 2000s when he first laid eyes on a raw youngster named Todd Carney.

'We had a very smart recruitment manager back then by the name of Dave Hamilton and he said to me, "I really want you to have a look at this kid—he is something special,"' Elliott, then head coach of the Raiders, recalls.

'We went to some small park—I cannot remember where—and he just carved them up playing for the Goulburn Stockmen at the age of around twelve or thirteen.

'He was on contract to us and I was in awe of his talent for one so young—but talent can be an overrated thing in our game.

'Plenty of young blokes have talent but those that go on to become champions, or even regular first-graders, are the ones who are prepared to work hard—and Todd had that in him from an early age. Partly because of his own ambition and partly because it was really instilled in him by his dad.

'He wasn't the best trainer early on and there were plenty of times when he had to do "extras" before or after training. But he accepted that and got stuck in and full credit to him for that. He realised he had to work harder and gritted his teeth and did it, and that is why he became such a dynamic player on the field. That first day, the thing that really impressed me—apart from the way he carved up the opposition on the field—is that he came up and said hello and chatted to Dave and me. Not many kids that age would do that.

'And not in a cocky way—just to thank us for coming along and showing interest in him. I was excited by what I saw. I could tell he was headed for big things.'

Fast forward to 2004, and Elliott handed the then seventeen-year-old Carney his top-grade debut.

'It was a big ask for such a young kid, to not only play first grade but to steer a team around the park as halfback,' Elliott explains. 'But he was ready, and while there were a few stumbles in that first season, he won our Rookie of the Year award and everyone predicted a bright future for him.'

A former youth worker in the rough area of Sydney around Kings Cross, Elliott understands tearaways like Carney better than most.

'He was no angel, but he wasn't the thug that a lot of people who don't know him like to portray him as,' Elliott says. 'He was a good kid who just did some bad things—and plenty of us have gone through that phase of doing silly things as kids. When I was at the Raiders and he started, we were fortunate to have senior players like Ruben Wiki, Clinton Schifcofske, Jason Smith and Simon Woolford at the club. They just had to look at you—when the boys were out in a group—and you would know to pull your head in if you were doing something wrong or over the top.'

Unfortunately for Carney, Elliott left for Penrith in 2007 and many of those senior players also moved on. 'The club lost a lot of experience all at once and young blokes like Toddy were suddenly without that guidance that they needed—on the field, but more importantly, off it. With the old heads there, if he ever got reckless, it wasn't tolerated. He knew where he stood because Jason Smith and Ruben would pull him into line very quickly and he respected and admired them. But they left, I left, he had problems at home and suddenly he had free rein to do what he liked. When his dad died, it stood out like dogs' balls to me—that was when his behavioural issues really became a problem.

'He suddenly got a bunch more tattoos and had anger and rage—it's a common reaction to the loss of a loved one at that age. His dad was a good guy who loved and cared about his son. Whenever I had talks with Todd about his future, Daryl was there. He was a huge influence in his son's life and suddenly that was gone. He was lost and rudderless and acted out. I'd seen it before and really felt for the kid. Surely I wasn't the only one seeing what was happening—I'm not that smart. But the thing is Todd wasn't bashing people or doing anything to women. Take a look at everything he did back in his dark days and there was only one victim of his silly acts—and that was Todd Carney.'

Elliott took the unprecedented step of calling the Raiders, even though he was now head coach of rivals Penrith. 'I won't name names but I spoke to a senior figure there because they needed to understand why Toddy was acting the way he was and get him back on track before things really escalated,' he says. 'I was told by Canberra in no uncertain terms to butt out and mind my own business. And in fairness, I can sort of understand where the Raiders were coming from. What I was doing may have been inappropriate, being coach of a rival club, but I cared a lot for the kid and felt I could help. I was worried about the direction his life was going in and was hopeful we could head it off and steer him back onto the right path. His behaviour went south after he lost his dad and we as a sport did not recognise that.'

Elliott remained a sounding board for Carney throughout his career and the pair are firm friends to this day. And Elliott believes the talented playmaker was crucified by the powers that be, who hounded him out of the game after the infamous 'bubbler' incident at Cronulla in 2014. 'I have to put my hand up and say I am not impartial here. Todd and I have plenty of history and I like the guy a lot,' he says. 'But the punishment—which effectively ended his career—didn't fit the crime. Yes, he has to take responsibility for his actions and there are consequences for bad behaviour. But take a look at what has been happening in rugby league over the past twelve months and clearly something is very wrong. A minority of players keep repeating acts that we as a society do not tolerate. The NRL is pouring a lot of resources into mental health and education but it is obvious that it is not working. Players continue to do the wrong thing—with women, with alcohol and with other issues, and a lot of it is preventable. Also, plenty of players are being whipped with a feather, and then you see the harsh punishment Todd got for what amounted to a stupid prank—it doesn't sit well with me. His NRL career is over now and he is older and wiser. He hasn't tried to shift the blame for his acts onto others—he has taken ownership of them and that is a good thing. With maturity comes a better understanding of yourself and your place in the world. Todd has turned his life around. He has learned the hard way, but he has learned. He's never been in the sort of denial that we often see from others in similar circumstances.'

Elliott's regret is that the game never saw the best of Todd Carney on a regular basis because of his foolish actions.

'He was an amazing talent,' Elliott, now a commentator and motivational speaker, laments. 'And the sad part is, he could have been a perfect senior player at any number of clubs now. I'm sad for Todd and I'm sad for our sport because we missed seeing a great player for several years at his peak. He had it all—speed, strength and football awareness—he was some player. He was a genuine footballer who played what he saw in front of him and had the confidence and class to come up with the big plays that win games. There aren't many of those players around. He could have been one of the elite play-makers of the modern era and it is heartbreaking really that we couldn't help him stay on the straight and narrow. Todd would have had a fantastic career but is now remembered for a lot of wrong reasons and things that could have been avoided with proper care.'

3

SMITHY SAILS IN

In 2005, a significant event happened at the Raiders with the return of Jason Smith from England. 'Smithy' was at the tail end of his career but his arrival was a great thing for the club. He was the ultimate professional and could read a game so well, with so much time with the ball in his hands, which I believe is the sign of a real class player. He was a boyhood hero of mine and I was thrilled that he was on board at the Raiders.

Right from his first session at pre-season training, Smithy added something to the team, and I was like a sponge, learning off him and getting the benefit of his vast experience. I felt I was in for a big year and I thrived playing off the back of him. Looking back on my career, I found that when I played on the back of dominant halves—guys like Smithy, Mitchell Pearce (at the Roosters) and Jeff Robson (Sharks)—it freed up my game and gave me a bit more time and space, which I was often able to capitalise on. I was to be the leading try scorer at the Raiders in the following two seasons and I put a lot of that down to Smithy's influence—he was great for me and my development into a regular first-grade NRL player capable of winning games. I was almost in a fullback role at times that season. I would come from deep and follow Smithy around the park and he would put me into holes.

This proved to be a turning point in my career because coach Brian Smith obviously noticed. A few years down the track, at my first training session with the Roosters in 2010, Brian came up to me and said simply, 'You'll be playing fullback. I think that is your best position because it gives you space to work in and use your pace.'

I ended up playing eleven games in 2005 and scored my first try in the NRL—that's a thrill for every player and a moment I will never forget. It came on a night where the Canberra spirit really shone through, against a Cowboys' team headed for the top eight, whereas we were down near the bottom of the ladder and ravaged by injuries. Matty only had nineteen fit players in the club to pick from during the week and many of the guys took the field with painkilling needles. I darted over for the opening try of the game and that silenced the capacity crowd in Townsville, and we led for much of the night, before our injury woes caught up with us. With a full house cheering them on, the Cowboys came home with a wet sail, edging us out 31–28. But there was a lot of pride in our sheds for the way we fought so hard in a game when we were in great difficulty and had nothing to play for, our season over with just one more game to play before Mad Monday. I remember Smithy, who played with a broken hand, telling us in the rooms afterwards, 'I've never seen a more courageous effort.' Coming from a bloke with his experience, it was a massive rap and Matty was also full of praise for our effort, even though we just fell short.

My goal in 2005 had been to become a better player than in my debut season and find some more consistency. I wanted to earn the confidence of my teammates as the guy in the number seven jumper.

I had a very good season in reserve grade that year and playing well there boosted my confidence for the games Matty called me in to first grade. I made most of the rep teams from reserve grade that season, including the Junior Kangaroos for the annual clash against Papua New Guinea. It was my first trip to PNG—the only country that calls league its national sport—and what an experience it was. The passion of the people has to be seen to be believed. I had a big game up there, scoring twenty points, which I believe is a record for that fixture. That season I had become used to playing against grown men in the NRL, so going back to reserve grade and junior footy suddenly was much easier for me, as that game showed.

•

I worked hard on my kicking game that year and particularly the 40–20 kick, which can prove a massive momentum shifter in games. To be able to kick the ball far downfield and then regain possession is a huge play and I found I had the ability to produce them on a fairly regular basis. When your forwards are tired it can really lift them, as well as getting the other team on the back foot. You have to be patient and pick your time, but I found it became a strength of mine and I worked hard on it before and after training. In several seasons, both in the NRL and Super League in Europe, I was the leading 40–20 kicker in the game and I took a lot of pride in that. Occasionally I would shank one and look like a goose when it went out on the full, which gave the opposition good field position from tackle one, but that is the risk you take. I grew in confidence in this area of my game and became known as something of a 40–20 sharpshooter. To this day, some of my mates call me '40–20' because that was a real trademark of my game.

Our 2006 season at the Raiders is best remembered for our golden point wins and I still get goosebumps when I think of them. Golden point is the ultimate pressure for any player and the ultimate high or low. You win a game that way and the feeling is a mixture of relief, joy and delight. You lose that way and it is just shattering. You put in all that effort, build yourself up for extra time, come so close . . . and then come away with nothing and watch on as the other team jumps up and down and hooplas.

We were lucky enough to have three golden point games go our way that year—all with me kicking clutch field goals—as we stormed into the finals against the predictions of the critics, many of whom predicted us finishing with the wooden spoon in January. The one that really stood out for me was against the Cowboys up in Townsville. It was a massive game for both teams played before a full house of parochial North Queenslanders. We went into extra time locked together on the scoreboard and it was very tense, with finals places up for grabs. Often in extra time you see players snap at field goals from ridiculous angles in a desperate attempt to break the deadlock. Well, that was me in Townsville that night. I got the ball a long way out—probably 45 metres—and thought there was no way I could make the distance. But it was last tackle and all or nothing. I struck it sweetly, it just snuck over the crossbar, and we came away with a vital win. The boys swamped me as the ball sailed over and it made the long trip back home much more enjoyable than usual. Matty put us on a curfew after the game to make sure we didn't go crazy. Me and a few of the boys started to make our way back to the team hotel from the pub around midnight, but as we did, we noticed Matty and a few of his mates—he was from Townsville—enjoying themselves in a local nightspot. So we headed straight for the nearest bar and broke curfew . . . if it's good enough for the coach to do it, we figured it was good enough for us to do the same.

That field goal was a rare moment of perfection and when we watched the video during the week, the coaching staff or other players would sometimes ask 'What made you think to pull that play off then?' And I struggle to answer them. The best answer I can come up with when I pull off a great play is that I *don't* think, I just do it. You train hard for those moments and are just in the zone and sometimes it comes off. Of course, the coach will ask the same question, with a different tone of voice, when you throw an intercept or kick a ball out on the full. Again, it's hard to describe the thought process—you just try to come up with the right play at the right time. It's instinct, and sadly sometimes it lets you down and you feel like crap for costing your teammates a possible win.

I kicked another pressure field goal late in the year against the Tigers in what was John Skandalis's last game. I still feel a little bad about raining on 'Skando's' parade. He was a great player for many years for the Tigers and I know how much the loss would have hurt. But that's footy: you win some, you lose some and you have to accept that or it will do your head in.

Field goals were similar to 40–20s in my mind—clutch plays that can win or lose a game. As a halfback and play-maker it is your job to nail them and I took a lot of pride on those occasions when I was able to get them over and win the game for the boys.

That 2006 season was definitely my breakout year in the NRL and as I said, I owed a lot of that to Smithy and his experience and calming influence. I felt 2006 and 2007 were the years I was in my prime at Canberra. I'd found my confidence, I had good players around me and I felt like I was making the team my own as playmaker out there in the middle. I was also still young enough to play Junior Kangaroos and at the end of the season, I was named captain of the team, which was a career highlight and I took massive pride from it.

•

Sadly 2006 ended on a sour note when I had my first brushes with the law. I was suddenly making good money and, as young blokes do, I wanted to spend it. I went out and one of the first things I bought was a bright orange Nissan Skyline. One weekend shortly before Christmas, Mum and Dad went on a trip away to Batemans Bay so I had some mates around for a party out at their property. We all had a bit too much to drink and before too long, one of my mates took the car for a spin around the neighbour-hood. Soon afterwards I did the same, probably driving a bit too quick but not causing any accidents. I put the car back in the garage and we got on with the partying and the drinking.

About twenty minutes later, a couple of cops knocked on the door and asked if I had been driving the car. They said some neighbours had recognised me driving a bit errat-ically and reported it to them. They took me down to the police station and breathalysed me there, and of course I was over the limit. They didn't breathalyse me at the scene or at the time I was driving, so I probably could have had the charges thrown out, but I was still a naive kid and next thing I knew, they'd tossed me in a cell for a few hours. It was dark by the time Mum and Dad arrived at the cop shop to bail me out. That was the thing I felt worst about: I had ruined their holiday and they had to come home early to get their son out of jail.

I expected Dad to give me a clip over the ear for being such a goose but it never came. He was relatively cool about it all and, looking back, that should have been my first warning sign that something wasn't quite right with him. Dad was always very strict with me and quick to jump all over me when I screwed up, but the hiding I was expecting never came. As a result, I thought I could get away with stuff and the worst period of my life entered full swing.

I appeared in court at Goulburn and was fined $2000 and banned from driving for five years as well as being placed on a three-year good behaviour bond. Luckily for me, I only registered a mid-range blood alcohol level of 0.145. The magistrate said that if I had gone over 0.15, just one more beer, I would have landed in jail. 'If you had returned a high-range reading, I would have had no hesitation in sending you to jail,' Magistrate Geraldine Beattie told me. 'You have let yourself, your club and the wider community down. If you breach the bond I am about to impose, you'll be back before me looking squarely at a jail sentence.'

I realised much of my bad behaviour happened back home in Goulburn with my old mates, so I virtually barred myself from the town and tried to stay in Canberra in my down time. It was a big step because my family was there, but Mum and Dad and my sisters came to Canberra to see me. If I did go to Goulburn, I made sure I was on my way back to Canberra before it got dark.

But for all this, there were still few consequences for my actions from the man I feared and respected most, my dad. I tried to walk the right line and most of the time I did, but I had lapses and my actions began to snowball, particularly when I was on the drink with my mates. I was not proud of it, and I did some idiotic and reckless things that embarrassed both myself and my family and painted the Raiders and footy in general in a bad light. But I had an immature attitude and seemed intent on self-destruction. I'm not looking for excuses—I've got no one to blame but myself. I should have known better, but I was a silly kid who achieved success all too easily and early, and with my dad's mind fading away, I didn't get the guidance I needed.

The court had banned me from driving for that initial offence, but of course that wasn't going to stop me getting behind the wheel.

•

Not long after that I bought my first apartment in Bruce, not far from the Raiders' training ground. A mate did the tiling of the bathroom and kitchen and called to tell me it was all finished. I was at the pub at the time and had had a few, but was excited at the prospect of seeing it. So I convinced my clubmate Steve Irwin to drive me in his ute to pay the guy first. Steve drank some more beers while he was there and thought he might be over the limit, so I offered to drive.

It was a stupid idea, but I was silly and dying to go and see the place done up. As I drove around a bend, the back wheels spun out a bit but I regained control of the car. Seconds later though, I saw a police car and panicked. I didn't have a driver's licence and had probably had a beer or two too many. Instead of stopping as any sensible bloke would, I decided to do a runner. I hit the accelerator and tried to lose the cops.

It was one of the dumbest things I have ever done and after a few minutes, Steve and I found ourselves in a dead-end street with the cops on our tail. I made a run for it and got away but Steve with his injured knee was left behind. The cops took him away and he explained that I had been driving the car.

Meanwhile, I was hiding up a tree. After calling my manager, Dave Riolo, I decided to go home to Mum and Dad as soon as possible and lie low. The cops went to my place looking for me but my flatmate Tom Witcombe told them I wasn't there and that he hadn't seen me, which was the truth.

A friend of mine drove me to Mum and Dad's house in Goulburn—my go-to place most times I got into strife in those early years at Canberra. It was awful having to face them and tell them what I had done, but I knew I had to do it. Mum almost threw up—she couldn't believe it and was so upset. Again, I expected a bollocking from Dad but he just kind of laughed.

The next morning, Mum drove me back to Canberra and I turned myself in at the police station. I was pretty much shitting myself but the cops were cool. A couple of them giggled about it and asked why I did a runner. I explained that I was terrified about being caught driving without a licence and the field day the media would have at me being in trouble yet again.

A month or so later, I pleaded guilty to a bunch of charges at the ACT Magistrates Court, including failing to stop when directed by police, negligent driving and driving while disqualified. I was told that a jail term was on the cards, but the judge went easy on me. He fined me $500, put me on a twelve-month good behaviour bond and banned me from getting behind the wheel for another five years, as well performing 200 hours of community service. He did put the fear of God into me, saying if I put another foot out of place, I would undoubtedly go to jail. Canberra fined me $20,000 and I was stood down for several matches.

I was embarrassed and my family suffered too with my sisters copping shit in the street—that was a low blow. The thought of jail terrified me. Losing football was devastating enough but being locked in a cell would have sent me round the bend. I went to see a psychologist to try to work through my problems and I lost five kilos in just a few weeks through not being able to eat or sleep properly. I was something of a joker but clearly didn't know where the boundaries of acceptable behaviour lay.

The guy I really felt sorry for was Steve. The club threw the book at him, seeing he was caught at the scene of the crime, and sacked him. They alleged he'd had a couple of prior incidents. I don't know if that is true or not, but there was no way he should have been sent packing for something that was my fault. He kind of disappeared after that and I never got the chance to say sorry to him, which I have always regretted. His career in the NRL was over and it was my fault—I felt a real dog.

Naturally Steve wasn't happy—no other club would pick him up after all the bad publicity and he lashed out in an interview in Brisbane's *Sunday Mail* not long afterwards.

'Mud does stick and that's the reason I want people to know the truth,' Irwin said. 'What has upset me is the Raiders saying that I've been guilty of prior offences. The fact is I've never been fined, I've never been reprimanded,

I've never had a written warning for anything and they are saying I had previous offences. I've been in trouble for not turning up to training with the right attitude, but there was never an off-field problem. At the end of the day, all you've got is your name and mine has been dragged through the mud. It's blown my reputation out of the water. Todd Carney got 200 hours community service and a $500 fine. I've lost $80,000 and a career in the NRL. I know who's getting looked after.'

Steve claimed it was double standards. The Raiders hit back by accusing him of not taking his rehabilitation on his knee seriously. But Steve was clearly angry and was having none of that. In the same article he slammed the club's excuse. 'As for not doing my rehab properly, seven months ago I complained that my knee was making noises. The Raiders' medical staff said it's part and parcel of having a reconstruction,' he told the paper.

"I've got [an independent] surgeon's report saying my knee is stuffed and even he said, "Your knee is f---ed". How can they not pick up on it? I physically couldn't do the rehab because it was too sore. That was the reason why I'm not playing.

'I felt they used me up to save Todd. I said I'd go to the players association, then [Raiders chief executive] Don

Furner said, "Well, we'll go to court". I couldn't afford to pay court costs, so I asked for a full release.'

As I said, I felt really sorry for Steve and wish I could make it up to him in some way. It should have been a sobering message to me that my actions had consequences for other people, but I was still a silly young bloke in party mode and it didn't sink in as fully as it should have.

For my part, I went to work in a factory for a few months packing CDs into cases as part of my punishment. It was menial work but taught me a valuable lesson. I was working with a bunch of other young guys and none of them knew who I was, and that was fine by me. Quite a few of the people I worked with had disabilities and it was a good lesson for me. They were good guys and made me more appreciative of how lucky I was to be healthy and a gifted athlete. When footy came up during chats in our lunch breaks, I told them I played for the team they supported, but I don't think any of them believed me, and I was okay with that. I was happy to be anonymous, take my medicine and stay out of the limelight.

Not being able to play football was by far the worst part of my punishment. For all I knew my career was over. I got depressed, barely ate or slept—it was like a nightmare I couldn't wake up from. The Goulburn Stockmen were good to me. They snuck me a key to their home ground and I trained there in the semi-dark after everyone went home. I'd have people say to me, 'Do you realise there's 10,000 people out there wanting to be in your position. Don't you realise how lucky you are?' All I could do was say I was sorry and that I would try to regain my reputation and standing in the game. I just didn't know if I would ever get the chance to—my career was really in the balance.

I had a cousin who was a fair bit older than me, Dean Mallott. He was from Goulburn and played in the Raiders junior league in the late 1980s and early '90s. They reckon he was going to be a superstar but fell foul of the law and spent time in jail more than once, and it ruined his career. Dean went from a child prodigy to a bloke who never played a first-grade match. We would chat but he never wanted to discuss what had happened to him. Talking to Dean helped me wake up to myself a bit, though. At that early stage of my career I was scared that I could turn out to be the person who sits at the end of a bar saying 'I could have been this or I could have been that'.

Around this time the Raiders realised I had some serious issues to cope with and sent me to counselling. It helped a little to have someone to vent to. I remember I had so much stuff bottled up inside and my first session lasted four hours. Dad had been diagnosed with dementia a couple of months earlier. He was only in his fifties and it was a shock to everyone. We knew something was wrong and he was slipping away from us. I had trouble accepting it and I think I was in denial.

Mum had taken him to a doctor, who said it was a mid-life crisis and that we shouldn't worry. Dad used to call me several times a day to talk footy, but over a short space of time he went into his shell, his own little world, and didn't ring at all. Again, I'm not making excuses, but stuff like that is hard when it is not just your dad but your coach, mentor and role model all rolled into one.

Mum really saved me from going crazy during the time I was barred from playing, and would ring literally every half hour to make sure I was okay. She knew what a toll it was taking on me and was determined to get her son over this hurdle and help get my life back on track. Mum also went onto the front foot, approaching both the club and the media, begging for some leniency due to the problems with Dad.

'There are some things that have happened with his father recently and he has been really troubled by them,' she told Sydney's *Daily Telegraph*. 'His father has been his coach, hero and mentor and he has taken it very badly. It hasn't come to the surface yet but I will be bringing it up with the club. Todd has been really struggling with what has happened. He did the wrong thing and I can't make excuses for it but you have to remember he is still just a kid. He panicked and did the wrong thing but then he did turn himself in [to police]. It would be a great shame if he had to leave the club. He has dreamed about playing for the Raiders since he was three years old. He has made a mistake but he will learn from it. I am hoping we can work something out and get him the help he needs.'

The press got stuck into me and I probably deserved it, although I was an easy target at that time. In the *Daily Telegraph*, the same paper, veteran journo Ray Chesterton wrote: 'Carney obviously needs to face some harsh realities about adulthood. He has been stupid, irresponsible and indifferent to social demands in the past. Twenty-somethings can be like that.'

One thing that gave me heart was that the senior leadership player group had a meeting and backed me. 'The club spoke to the senior leadership group and, as players, we didn't want to see Todd let go,' prop Troy Thompson told the media. 'The team needs him and the club needs him. He's going okay but he is still very embarrassed. He is going to get better but everyone is worried about him going to jail.' Ultimately, the club listened to the senior players and reinstated me after a period away from the game.

As if all this wasn't bad enough, the 2007 season was a troubled one on the field for the Raiders. Jason Smith left the club for a final season at the Cowboys and his departure hit us hard. We went back to a younger half-back combination of me with Terry Campese, or Michael Dobson at times. It was a learning curve and we struggled without Smithy and some of the other senior guys who left. Every club goes through these rebuilding years from time to time—even powerhouses like the Roosters or the Broncos—and it was our turn to face the music. We also had a new coach in Neil Henry and took a while to adapt to his style of play. Matty had left to go to Penrith and I'd be lying if I said I didn't miss him. And that was nothing against Neil—he was a smart coach and he tried hard to get us firing. It just didn't happen, and it's disappointing for all concerned because you go out and bust your gut but, ultimately, you don't get the wins the fans crave and people start looking for excuses and scapegoats.

After sitting out of the game for the longest and hardest seven weeks of my life to that point, the Raiders thought I had served my time and Neil Henry picked me in the NRL again—to face the Tigers in Canberra. Sadly by then the season was slipping away from us. We had lost three of our last four games and confidence in the camp was shot. Losing, just like winning, is contagious and we had caught the bug. We put up a good fight against the Tigers but I was short of a gallop and still down on myself. We got beaten 16–22. It was in the middle of a miserable run: we won just three of our final eleven games and finished the season third last on the ladder. We beat only Newcastle and the Panthers home and won just nine of our 24 games.

Individually, I thought I still had a pretty good season. I was the club's top point scorer and top try scorer, so that was pleasing. Ultimately, though, it was my job to get the team over the line in the close games and, without Smithy to show the way, I was still too young to do that on a consistent basis in 2007. Footy can be a cruel game sometimes and that year I—and the team as a whole—got found out after our success of the previous year. We weren't able to ambush teams the way we did in 2006 and in my memory, 2007 was a year of frustration.

THE SISTERS

Krysten and Melinda admit that carrying the surname Carney hasn't always been easy. 'When Todd was in trouble at different times it was always a tough time on him and his family. It was hard for us to be there for him and to give him the good talking-to he needed,' Melinda says. 'There was always so much media attention and negative publicity which was quite harsh and cruel. He wouldn't want us to come to him as he didn't want us to have to face the media circus. Plus they would be at his house and trying to take photos of him through windows. They followed his every move, which made it hard to give him a good talking-to at the time of his actions and be cranky with him. We needed him to know we were there for him and supported him, as we would be fearful for his mental health and how he was dealing with the publicity. Despite his reputation, he is a sensitive guy and once he sobered up and realised the impact of his actions, he was really hurting inside and embarrassed by what he had done. Apart from the drink-driving charge, the things that Todd did wrong or attracted bad attention for were stupid decisions that hurt himself and his career—not anyone else. But it was always blown up like he had murdered someone and he was made out to be the worst person in the world. We would basically just try not to watch the news or read media reports and stay away from social media, as some of the comments were very hurtful. And they all came from keyboard warriors who had never met him and wanted to just kick the poor guy when he was down.

'At games, it is sometimes really hard for us to hold our tongues when idiots in the crowd abuse him. They are entitled to their opinions, of course, but yelling nasty remarks is just mean. Both of us girls are more outspoken than Todd—he just shrugs off the haters. We would love to give them a piece of our minds, but imagine if the media got hold of that. It would just add fuel to the fire so we try to ignore it and are just thankful that our kids were too young to understand the horrible things people were saying about their uncle. Our husbands have said a few words to fans in the crowd when the comments got too over the top, however. These idiots don't seem to realise, or care, that these players are just human beings, like everyone else, who have feelings, who make mistakes . . . and who have families who love them. Even at work, Krysten and I both deal with customers and sometimes the subject of Todd Carney and his antics will come up. They will have a crack at him—not real-ising who we are—and again, we just try to bite our tongues.'

The family went through their worst times when father Daryl rapidly went downhill with dementia. 'We could tell there was something wrong with him, living with him daily in Goulburn,' Krysten says. 'Todd was a bit sheltered from it all, living in Canberra and always being busy with football, which may have been a good thing for him because it was a very tough period for all of us. Mum took [Dad] to all sorts of doctors trying to find out what was wrong until they finally diagnosed the dementia, and it was devastating for us all. We tried to shield Todd from it because we knew it would destroy him inside, but he soon noticed there was something wrong—even in Canberra. Dad used to ring him countless times a day to ask about training and to talk about games—all of a sudden that stopped. He lost interest in his career and going to Todd's games and that is when Todd really came to understand that there was something very wrong with his dad.

'At the times when Todd came home, he could see how much his father was deteriorating and we could see how it was eating away at him inside. He was almost in denial, still mucking around with Dad and joking with him the way they used to when Dad was well. But that Daryl was long gone, sadly, and at times he was almost scared of Todd when he was fooling around with him—it was hard for all of us to watch. We explained to Todd that Dad was a different person now, that the guy who brought him up and coached him for all those years and mentored him on and off the field was no longer there, and Todd had trouble coming to terms with it. It was around then that he started to act out and when he got in trouble for drink driving in Canberra, Dad didn't say a word to him. That really hit home to Todd. We are certain that Todd lost his way because of all this, but he is the type of guy who would never look for excuses or blame his bad behaviour on Dad's illness.

'The Raiders sacked [Todd] and then he was denied a visa to England. That was another blow but in hindsight it was a blessing as we had him home to be together in Dad's final months in 2008. Todd got the chance to see Dad daily as [he] deteriorated rapidly in these months, going downhill before our eyes. You have no idea how hard it was to see our beloved Dad, our strong hero and role model, suffer this way—it's such a cruel disease. We feel for all families who have to go through this with a loved one. I know Todd has donated money to dementia research whenever he can in the hope that a cure is found so that other families can avoid our heartache. Even when he was sick, we never imagined that one day it would come to an end and we would lose Dad, not even on his last day when Mum called us together to go to the hospital. The doctor warned us that things didn't look good but somehow it still didn't sink in as we all sat around his bed. Then, suddenly he was gone, peacefully in his sleep, mercifully. But for us left behind to pick up the pieces, it still rocks us as much now as it did on that terrible day.

'Because Todd and Dad had such a close bond, he struggled with it more than anyone. It was around that time that he jumped on a car bonnet during one of his nights out—clearly frustrated and angry at life—and got banned from Goulburn and sent up to Atherton. It was that or jail so the choice was a simple one . . . but for a kid grieving the loss of his dad, to be sent so far away, it was really hard on him. He doesn't talk about it much or complain because that is the kind of guy Todd is—he accepts his punishment and gets on with life. But Mum knew how much her little boy was hurting and she went up and visited whenever she could. Eventually she moved up there full-time for the last six months of his stay there, she was so worried about him. And he was staying with a loving, caring family who took him in—the Nassers—but he still clearly was struggling with his dad gone and his mum so far away.'

4

BACK ON TRACK

We started 2008 as hot favourites for the wooden spoon but, as can happen at Canberra, we exceeded expectations by a long way. The Knights beat us in Round 1, but we learned plenty from that and won three of our next four games to give us some momentum for the long road ahead. I really started to attract media attention after probably my best game to date in April of that year, against the Tigers. In a see-sawing match in Canberra, I scored the winning try in a thriller, 30–24.

The press started talking me up as a representative player and I got a run for Country Origin against City, which was a nice nod of recognition for my form from the selectors.

I put my form down to a lot of hard work in the video room. Scott Prince was at the top of his game for the Titans, Queensland and Australia that year and I spent a lot of time studying him, watching how he controlled games and floated in and out of play, always making an impact when he chose his moment to strike.

We had a stack of injuries mid-season and everyone expected us to fold, but Neil Henry was a smart coach and he managed to get the best out of us. We beat the Broncos at home in Round 14 and the following week racked up 58 points against the Bulldogs—their heaviest defeat in over 50 years. Our attack was capable of being white hot and we put 74 points on Penrith one afternoon in August and finished the regular season in a very creditable sixth spot.

We came up against a strong Cronulla side in the first week of the finals, and they towelled us up 36–10 at home, but we thought we would get a second bite of the cherry in the McIntyre System. The next day, in a massive upset, the eighth-placed Warriors knocked off minor premiers Melbourne and we were out, which was devastating after such a good season. We didn't see it coming, as the Storm were certainties at home, and it was a long, painful off-season while we contemplated what might have been.

I was coming off contract at the end of 2008 and had never thought for a second about leaving the Raiders. There were plenty of stories in the media about the big money rival clubs were throwing at me and fans swamped social media begging me to stay, which I was quite humbled by. But Matty's departure got me thinking and he made me an offer to join him at Penrith, which I thought long and hard about. I went and saw Panthers' supremo Phil 'Gus' Gould out there and said to him tongue-in-cheek (sort of), 'I don't know any of your players . . . I won't have anyone to have a drink with.' He gave me that sly grin of his and said, 'That's the idea.' But that wasn't the reason I said 'no' to Gus and the Panthers—I just didn't fancy living out in Sydney's far west at Penrith, so far from home and family.

I also got a very tempting offer from Manly and they were a powerful team at that stage. I went and visited their facilities at Brookvale and sat down with Des Hasler—and agreed to play for the Sea Eagles in 2009. It wasn't an easy decision but he painted a great vision and Manly were a top club with big name players and a history of success.

I got back to Canberra and told them of my decision and immediately the heat was on. Neil Henry called me into his office and told me he had agreed to extend his time at the club and I was a big part of his plans, saying no way could I let him down and leave. He had worked with Johnathan Thurston in his previous stint as an assistant coach at the Cowboys and thought I could go to a similar level as 'JT' under his guidance. Next thing I knew, my phone rang—and it was Mal Meninga on the line. Mal was a boyhood hero and is, of course, a Canberra and rugby league legend. He told me the club had a massive future and that they valued me greatly. He also told me how proud he was to have been a one-club player in his time and that after my career was over, I would feel the same way if I stayed true to the Raiders. So I caved—the pressure got to me.

I agreed to stay at Canberra and had the daunting task of ringing Des and telling him I had changed my mind. I didn't know what to expect, as Des had a reputation of being a bit fiery and he had every right to give me a blast. But when I called, to my great relief, he was understanding. 'You're still a young bloke and they got to you—I get it,' Des said. 'Maybe we can work together at other clubs in the future.' He left it at that, and more than once in the subsequent years Des made me offers and we came close to agreeing terms. It was a tough call, but the fans at Canberra had supported me and it would have been hard to just turn my back on them and leave.

Sadly, I quickly came to rue my decision. A week after assuring me he was staying at Canberra and would personally take my game to the next level, Neil Henry called me into his office. He said he had decided to leave to take up the position as head coach of the Cowboys. Neil was the major reason I had re-signed at the Raiders and I immediately felt very let down and used. With the benefit of hindsight, I should have taken that Manly offer. It was the right time to move on and I would have avoided what became a nightmare year at Canberra.

The 2008 season and year as a whole was a disaster for me. Dad died at the age of just 57, and I went into a downward spiral. Seeing him deteriorate from a healthy, happy man into a shell of a person broke all our hearts. Dementia is a horrible disease and I feel for all the families affected by it, like mine was. He was my coach and mentor from the age of six to sixteen and made me the player I was by pushing me to my limits. It was awful losing him but I think he is still looking over me, and in big games I felt his spirit pushed me that little bit harder, bringing out the best in me.

I can see now that I was in a state of shock. I couldn't believe I'd lost my dad at such a young age and felt he had been cut down in his prime. Coming on top of Pop dying a couple of years earlier, it was a terrible double blow and I'd lost the two men who meant most to me. Pop was like my stress relief—when footy and Dad got too intense, we'd go fishing and I'd de-stress. We had a special relationship. I can't remember either funeral—I just blocked them out, it was such a horrible time.

Without the two of them, I was a mess and started to wander aimlessly through life, quickly getting into more strife. One weekend I went out with the Raiders boys to a nightclub in Canberra, All Bar Nun. There was a bit of an altercation between me and some bloke who was a mate of our front-rower, Dane Tilse. Next thing I knew, the bloke had called the cops and alleged I had urinated on him. Because of my reputation, the cops took him at his word and I was in massive trouble again. They suspended me for two weeks and in the meantime, the guy told Dane that he would withdraw the charges if I paid him $5000. I thought all along he was trying to blackmail me and that's what it turned out to be. So I said 'okay' and he dropped the charges but I never gave him the cash. I wasn't about to give in to those kind of threats and what could he do—he couldn't go to the cops and say he didn't get his blackmail money after dropping the charges.

The guy was persistent, and he sent a strange letter to my manager Dave Riolo on 14 August 2008. In it he repeated his accusation and asked for an explanation why financial compensation had not been forthcoming, threatening further action. There was some more legal to-ing and fro-ing before he eventually dropped his frivolous claim.

But the club wasn't happy with all the bad publicity I had been generating. Raiders chairman John McIntyre told the media that I had 'problems in my head'. McIntyre added: 'He's certainly on a ban until we can get to the bottom of everything, he probably should put himself on a lifetime ban [from alcohol]. The thing they really love is playing, so it hurts them if they are unable to do so. I am not saying that's what we're going to do, but it is something that we will talk about. Whatever we do has to be in the best interests of the game and the best interest of the club and it might be a bit like what [former racehorse owner] Tony Hartnell did with Takeover Target. The only difference is that he had a horse that wasn't right in the leg and we've got a player who isn't right in the head.'

Chief executive Don Furner had advised my manager on 30 July—just one day after the incident and without me having an opportunity to defend my actions—that the board had met and stopped one step short of invoking a termination, instead offering the following conditions:

1. I was to be stood down for the remainder of the 2008 season.
2. I was to be removed from leadership group.
3. I was to undertake a professional course of counselling for my alcohol-related behaviour (not grief counselling, which would have helped me more, I believe).

4. I was to refrain from drinking alcohol until the end of my contract, which was the end of 2012.

5. In conformity with the club's responsibility for my welfare and personal development the board wanted me to undertake part-time work/volunteer work for the remainder of the 2008 season and 2009.

6. I was to be fined $20,000.

The rumour mill went into overdrive and I went from footballer to axe murderer in the eyes of a lot of the public. Exasperated, frustrated, angry, I didn't know what to do. So I took the unusual step of writing an open letter to the fans and releasing it to the media to tell my side of the story. Here's how it read:

> The purpose of this letter is to clarify some things to fans of the Canberra Raiders, Rugby League fans and the public in general.
>
> I feel I need to tell my side of the story regarding an incident at a Canberra pub on Sunday 20th July, after our win over the Roosters. It has been well documented that I was drunk and that an incident did occur in the toilets.
>
> I am extremely sorry for the incident which occurred, however I believe the details of that night have not been reported accurately. I was not running around (as some

would have you believe) urinating on patrons in the bar. The person involved was drinking in our group and whilst yahooing in the toilets, things got out of hand. The line between good fun and inappropriate behaviour was crossed.

It was not my intention to degrade or offend anyone and I have apologised to the fellow concerned. I am regretful of the incident and the ensuing media circus and am embarrassed at the unwanted focus on myself and the Club. Since this, I feel that 'every man and his dog' has a 'Todd Carney' story. My primary school sweetheart has emailed the Club and the media about the time I pulled her piggy tails! Not really, but it feels like an old-fashioned witch hunt.

Look, I am not an angel—far from it. I am a 22-year-old; I love my footy and having a good time. I am the first to admit that I have had some issues off the field—just Google me! I am also very aware that I have had some problems when drinking alcohol. I do not have an alcohol problem in needing to drink all the time or anything like that; more a problem with not handling myself in a proper manner on occasion when on the drink. I am addressing this issue to avoid future incidents.

Furthermore, whilst there have been some things I'm not proud of in the past, I don't get around barking at women or deliberately trying to antagonise people, contrary to some media reports. I also try to do my bit with promos, autographs and appearances in the Community etc.

In regard to the Canberra Raiders, I love the Club. I have played with them since I was twelve years old and recently knocked back a number of big money deals from other NRL clubs and overseas to sign a four year deal with the Club. On the whole, the Club has been very supportive of me throughout my career and helping with issues in the past.

However, I must say that I am disappointed with the way that this incident has been handled. I have read reports about my teammates having input into my punishment and I have not even been given the opportunity to address them or the coaching staff on my issues.

I was not present or invited to discuss the allegations with the Board, I was just handed a punishment through my Manager.

I am still committed to the Raiders, however I am appealing the process of these events in the hope that I can be back on the field in the lime green as soon as possible, if the Club allows it.

If my actions have caused hurt or embarrassment to my fans, family and friends as well as the Club, I am truly sorry.

While it got my message out there, it got me little sympathy from the people who really mattered—the big dogs at the Raiders and the NRL. Then NRL boss David Gallop got involved, declaring he would suspend me not just for the rest of 2008 but for all of the *next* season if I failed to follow the Raiders' six-point plan. And yet he was letting other blokes who did things far worse than me simply change clubs and play on. I was filthy and disillusioned.

A couple of days after Gallop spoke out, I went to Goulburn Workers Club to celebrate the 50th birthday of Chris Anthony, the father of one of my mates, Mitch. Some blokes on the drink spotted me and tried to start a fight and Mitch stepped in, telling them to just leave us in peace. Next thing, security stepped in and Mitch and a few other blokes were tossed out of the place. Because I was there it became a headline again, even though I didn't do a thing wrong. It was simply open season on Todd Carney. Chris was angry that my name was dragged through the ringer again and defended me in the press. 'I'm sick of people flinging mud at Todd that's just not true,' he said. 'It's a load of crap what's been reported. He had a couple of beers, that's all. He wasn't drunk. He's not that stupid. Give him some credit, the kid's no angel and he's had some troubles but the thing on Saturday night is a load of crap and the mud is sticking.'

After receiving Don Furner's email with the six-point plan there was an urgent disciplinary hearing with the club's board. After a long hearing my manager, Mum and I went to have a coffee and we decided that we would accept their plan, although we wanted to appeal against not playing for the rest of the season. But when we went back into the room, the board had all bolted except for one bloke, who told me they had decided to sack me instead and tear up my contract, which was worth around $400,000 a season.

Some Canberra fans are still dirty on me, believing I quit the club, but I feel the Raiders just cut me loose. I would have accepted their demands, including giving up the grog. I was devastated but thought I could do what other blokes in similar positions had done—pick up the pieces at another club and start again. But the NRL would have none of it and David Gallop came out and said that they would not register me at another club until the end of 2009 at the earliest.

I couldn't believe it. Could they do this? Was it in writing somewhere? Was I ever notified officially? I believe it was simply done by a handshake agreement between Gallop and the Raiders. The NRL de-registered me for one year after the Raiders called them and told them they had sacked me, effectively leaving me in limbo. This had never happened to any player in the history of the game before—it's almost a league tradition that if a club sacks you, you go somewhere else and start again. But for some reason, the NRL broke new ground with me.

The Players Association backed me, saying I had a right to play football at a new club as so many sacked players had done before me. But the NRL refused to budge. Lack of consistency in punishment has always been a problem at the NRL and they seemed determined to come down hard on me while other players—some of whom had committed far more serious crimes—were just given a slap on the wrist. I couldn't understand it. The Dragons were ready to sign me but as a result of the NRL ban, it didn't happen.

I was ready to go to Super League and try a change of scenery and a fresh start at Huddersfield where Nathan Brown was then head coach. I signed a three-year deal with the English club, having decided that a fresh start as far from Canberra and the NRL as possible was the best thing for me. I had my stuff all ready to go when I got a 3 a.m. phone call from the boss of Huddersfield. One thing I've learned in my life is that 3 a.m. phone calls are never good and this was no exception. 'I've got some bad news for you, lad—they've cancelled your visa.' I looked at my bags, all packed on the floor, ready to go the next day . . . I couldn't believe it. I had a police record, due to my criminal conviction in Australia, and they wouldn't let me into the UK. I learned years later that you can challenge those things, but back then I just accepted it.

NRL players who had done a lot worse than me had no trouble getting a start in the UK and getting the tick of approval from the immigration department over there. Yet for some reason, I was 'off limits' and the door was slammed in my face.

MUM

Todd and his grandfather were extremely close, Leanne Carney says. 'Lindsay developed lung cancer but he was a tough old bloke. Not even that would stop him going to games to watch Todd. He was so crook in his latter days but we'd call him and say "we are driving to Sydney to watch Todd play" and he would insist on coming along. He eventually died when Todd was around sixteen and it hit the kid hard. They loved each other and Lindsay was the voice of reason when Daryl was pushing him too hard . . . now he was gone.'

But much worse was to come for the Carney family as they slowly came to realise there was something very wrong with Daryl. 'The first clue I got was one day we were on a caravan holiday down the south coast,' she says. 'A man who we knew walked past and we asked how he was doing. He said, "Not so well—my wife died two weeks ago," and Daryl just started laughing. I couldn't believe it—it was just such an inappropriate and embarrassing thing to do.

'I started to notice other odd behaviour. One day a friend saw him driving, two cars behind me, following me to work. [Daryl] was convinced I was having an affair. Then he would ring me up at work and abuse me, saying awful things, that I was with another man and he would get us both and we'd be sorry. I was at a loss—it was so unlike him. I took him to a bunch of doctors—one said he was going through a mid-life crisis, another said he was depressed. One night at the dinner table he said something disgusting to me and Todd actually slapped him—it is probably the only time I have ever seen him hit anyone. Todd yelled, "Don't you talk to my mother like that." We were going through hell—he treated the kids and me like dirt.

'Football used to be his life, but he lost interest. Once I said to him, "Come on, let's go. Todd's playing." But he just said he wasn't going. I knew it would hurt Todd's feelings if his dad wasn't at the game so when we got to the ground and he asked where his father was. I told him Daryl had a crook stomach and wasn't up to the trip. So he decided to ring home and stir his old man up. But one of the girls answered the phone and when Todd wanted to talk to him she said, "The old bastard has gone to the pub." That shocked Todd. It really made him realise his dad had changed.

'Then one day I told my story to a psychiatric nurse who lived in our street. She had a hunch what was wrong and arranged for us to visit a brain injury unit. They did a bunch of tests on Daryl and found he had early onset frontal lobe dementia— he was only in his early fifties. It was a shock, but it was also an answer to the questions we had had for years and almost a relief. I thought my husband hated me. Now I understood it was all beyond his control. And by the time it was diagnosed the illness was at a fairly advanced stage. The doctor called us all in and said "Your father isn't your father anymore and your husband isn't your husband anymore." It was as simple as that. The girls seemed to accept it better than Todd . . . he really struggled. I think it may well have been caused by all the head knocks he got, both on the field and fighting outside the pub, but we will never know. I see there is a lot of research being done into concussion and the effect on sportsmen later in life and believe it was a factor for sure—it is very unusual for a guy in his fifties to go downhill so fast with dementia.

'While he and Daryl clashed on occasion, Todd knew that Daryl had made him the player he was—he coached him for ten years and pushed him to be the best he could be on the field. Plenty of players have talent and never use it, but Daryl ensured that Todd combined that talent with drive and desire, and that's why he got to the very top.

'The illness got worse and it got to the stage where we had to watch him for 24 hours a day. I remember there were times when Todd would have to look after him when I went to work. We wouldn't let him drive because he could have killed someone, but he wanted to get on the road. One day Todd called me and said, "The old bugger got in my car, didn't have the keys but he took off the hand brake and rolled it down the street." We eventually had to put him into care. He couldn't be left home alone and it was too much. He was a danger to himself. He was leaving the stove on and he started smoking—he could have burnt the house down. We would visit him but it all became too much for Todd. "I'm not going anymore," he said to me one day. "He doesn't even recognise me—he doesn't know who I am. It's just too hard and makes me too sad—it is doing my head in." Daryl passed away suddenly one day in 2008 in the nursing home, and even though we knew it was coming, it took us by shock. In just a few years, he'd gone from a fit, vibrant healthy man to this. It gave us all a lesson about how precious life is and that you need to treasure every day.

'I think Todd went off the rails after he had gone. Daryl was the guy who he feared and respected and would make sure he didn't stray far off track. With him gone, Todd lost himself and started being silly and reckless, and getting in trouble on a regular basis. It's like he didn't care about the consequences because the man who disciplined him had left us.'

Leanne blames the Raiders for rushing her son through the system. 'He moved there at seventeen and I cried all the way on the drive from Goulburn to Canberra,' she recalls. 'I felt like I was losing my boy. As we got closer to Canberra, Todd said to me, "Mum, you do know you're going to have to stop crying when we arrive—it will embarrass me."

'They put him straight into the first-grade squad—I wanted him to finish his schooling and take his time but he and his dad out-voted me. I've got a video of him at age three wearing a little Raiders jumper, in which he says to his cousin, "I'm going to play for this team one day," pointing to the shirt. That's how much the Raiders meant to him. But it was all too much, too soon for a naive young kid. They put him up at the Australian Institute of Sport with a few of the other young guys and he soon got homesick. He would often drive home to Goulburn at the end of the day's training to be with his family, then get up at 5.30 the next morning and drive back to Canberra. I had to call them up and tell them "He's struggling to fit in . . . he's just a shy country kid." They had no idea, and they really didn't seem to care too much. They saw potential in him as a footballer and that is all the club cared about. He was just a cog in the machine.

'Todd had bad acne on his back, because he was still a teenager, and he was embarrassed to take his T-shirt off. So when the team had swimming sessions, he would say he had a middle ear infection to get out of them, so he wouldn't have to take his shirt off. He was just thrown into the mix and there was no understanding that he was a raw seventeen-year-old kid. We didn't even let him start drinking until he was eighteen.

'Every time he screwed up in Canberra, they just whacked him with a fine or a suspension. There didn't seem to be any duty of care or understanding that he was still a kid who had lost his dad. Without that father figure, things spiralled quickly.

He missed out on a real childhood because his dad had been so strict on him, and he started acting out in his early twenties, doing the things he couldn't do as a fourteen-year-old. And if he did those silly pranks as a fourteen-year-old, people would have shrugged their shoulders and said "He's just a stupid kid". But all of a sudden he did them as a twenty-year-old football star and they became back page news.

'He has a problem with the drink—there's no way I'm going to deny that. You look at all the stuff he has been involved in and beer is the common denominator. We were very strict on him with alcohol as a kid and maybe then he was doing his best to catch up . . . I don't know! I've told him many times, "Todd, it's okay to have a wine or two with dinner or a beer or two at the pub and then go home." It does make me mad because the message obviously hadn't got through to him. I guess it's just the way he is wired. He will be good as gold for a while and then fall off the wagon. But he is older and more mature now—he turned 30 a couple of years ago. And he's not stupid. He has learned from his mistakes and I think the message has finally got through.

'Now he is out of the NRL bubble he has a better perspective about things. He is thinking about life after football and has plenty of plans to put back into the game and coach kids. He has a good heart and anyone who knows him will tell you that. He does a lot of charitable acts. But few people know about them because he doesn't want publicity for these actions, he just does it because he likes to help people out and enjoys making them smile. When he is back in Goulburn he will often pop in to the nursing home I work at, just to chat to the patients—it makes their day. And despite all the stuff that has gone down, most people in Canberra and Goulburn still love him and care about him. I often find it takes me five minutes to get into the local mall and half an hour to leave, because everyone is always asking me, "How is Todd doing?"'

But Leanne admits Carney's trouble and strife has made it hard for the family at times. 'When he's done something bad, we walk down the street and people give us funny looks,' she says. 'And I've told Todd that we are the ones who have to live with the consequences of his actions. I've heard so many people say "That Todd Carney—isn't he a dickhead!" I feel like saying to them "Have you ever met him? Do you know him?" And of course they haven't.

'The Todd Carney portrayed in the media is a very different person to the one we know and love. He would do anything for me and his sisters and we have got even closer since Daryl died. And I've got news for the critics—he's sane and level-headed now and planning his life out. If anything, his sisters are madder than him!' she laughs. 'I just wish every story about him in the media wouldn't start with the words "Bad boy". They don't stop to think he is a human being with feelings and a guy who has touched many lives. But then that never rates a headline.'

•

Without the football, my life began to unravel even further. A lot of the dumb things I did happened around the time of Dad's sickness and eventual death. The Raiders had treated all my punishments as alcohol-related, when the deep core was the trauma from Dad. These days, there are all sorts of mental health programs for players like me who go off the rails. But back then, there was nothing concrete like that set up and I found myself pretty much left to fend for myself. Like I've said many times, I'm not making excuses. I was young and reckless and have to put my hand up for my own irresponsible actions. Most of them revolved around alcohol, and without footy I went over the top with my drinking and, as a result, I was a loose cannon.

I couldn't take a trick either. Another scandal erupted. A woman who I had never met broke her phone so she went into a Telstra store and they gave her a 'lender' while hers was being repaired. Well, it happened to be an old phone of mine—and on it were a few explicit photos I had taken of myself in front of a mirror.

Again, I was young and silly, but a girl had sent me some lewd photos of herself so I did the same back. My fault again, but how dumb and irresponsible of Telstra to just give out a phone to someone without wiping the data off it?

The result was that the press found out about it, of course, and made a huge 'Camera catches out nude Carney' headline out of it. Telstra launched an internal investigation into the whole thing and someone probably got their butt kicked. Again, I had to call Mum and tell her about the whole thing. No mum should be put through all this stuff and I felt like the lowest bloke on earth.

•

Despite everything that had happened that year, I did have one amazing experience, shortly after the 2008 grand final. A few months earlier, former Raiders prop turned politician Paul Osborne took one of his kids to Africa to help the locals rebuild the country of Rwanda after all the internal battles and killing that had gone on for years there. A committed Christian, 'Ossie' likened his fourteen-year-old son to many NRL players—immature and out of touch with the realities of the adult world. He saw how much good the trip did for his son and thought it could work similar magic for footballers who lived their lives in a bubble.

So the man who is forever remembered as the unlikely hero of Canberra's 1994 grand final win, after he was brought in at the last moment by coach Tim Sheens, assembled a motley crew of players including Nathan Hindmarsh, Justin Poore, Todd Payten, Jared Waerea-Hargreaves . . . and yours truly. It didn't sound like my type of end-of-season trip at first, but Ossie talked me around. He said it would do me good to see how fortunate we are to live in a lucky country like Australia and helping the locals rebuild their lives would make me feel good about myself again.

My schedule wasn't exactly busy at the time so I thought, 'Why not?' But little did I realise what I was letting myself in for—probably none of us did. The morning after the grand final, we boarded a plane bound for Johannesburg. Two more flights, and 38 hours after we left Sydney, we finally arrived in the Rwandan capital, Kigali. It was dusty, dirty and poor, but I found the experience incredibly moving. I'd never heard of the place during my privileged upbringing in the New South Wales bush but soon got a lesson I would never forget.

Our job was to help build the Village of Hope, a home for the widows and children of men killed in the country's brutal 1994 genocide. They reckon almost a million people were murdered in a mad civil war, often hacked to pieces with axes and machetes. We went to visit a memorial and all of us were stunned at the cruelty, the inhumanity of the killings—how could people be so hateful to their fellow countrymen? I was at a loss. The Hutus basically ran the country and for no particular reason they decided to wipe the minority people, known as the Tutsis, off the face of the earth. Men, women and children—no one was spared.

At the memorial building there was one room which had a special exhibit to commemorate the lives of twelve murdered children. All the guys went and looked at it and were stunned—except Nathan Hindmarsh, who couldn't bring himself to go inside. I asked him why he skipped that part of the tour and he looked at me and said, 'Mate, I have two kids. I just can't look at that shit.'

We had a very rewarding time carting around bricks— or what pass for bricks in Rwanda—to the locals as they built houses for the women and children who survived the carnage. It was hard, physical work but gave me, gave us all, a real sense of satisfaction. It wasn't all work though, as we also trekked up the Congo River and got up close to some gorillas. They are magnificent beasts out in the wild. We also played a game of touch footy on a field full of potholes with a deflated ball against a local rugby union team. I could have done myself a serious injury on such a treacherous surface but I didn't care—it was the first time I'd played footy in months and I wasn't about to give up the chance. It just reinforced to me how much I missed the game.

The locals loved us being there and I am still in touch with one of the workers from the hotel we stayed at on Facetime when we get the opportunity. It was far from the Hilton, but the service was top notch.

Not all the people were quite so nice, though, as big Jared Waerea-Hargreaves found out one day. He went for a walk and a couple of the locals tried to mug him—not a smart move when you look at the size of the bloke. Not surprisingly, they finished worse for wear, but it was a timely reminder to us that we were strangers in a strange land.

Overall though, while I had my initial doubts, I'm glad I went and it was one of the most incredible experiences of my life.

•

Back home with no footy to keep me on the straight and narrow, it wasn't long before I was in the doghouse again—early in 2009 to be precise.

I was enjoying a night out with a mate at the Goulburn Workers Club and we staggered outside in the early hours of the morning after having a few sherbets too many. There were cars everywhere and, idiots being idiots, we didn't walk *through* the cars, we walked *over* the cars. It was called vandalism by the cops but it was really just stupidity and I don't think any cars were damaged. Then we got a kebab—as you do after too many drinks—and the kebab stand was outside a Fone Zone store. My mate kicked in the door of the store—why, I don't know—and then he bolted. I didn't even realise what he had done and was happily eating my kebab, sitting on the side of the road. The Goulburn cops, who knew me well by this stage, took one look at the smashed in door, one look at me, and next thing I knew I was in a cell. I was in there for around three hours, answering questions and just biding my time. It was a horrible feeling, especially as I had done nothing to the storefront. I didn't want to give up my mate to the cops, but in the end I didn't have to. Next morning, my mate sobered up and heard that I had been arrested for his moment of madness and he felt a rush of guilt. He went straight to the police station and fessed up to the crime.

The cops had a bit of a set against me—which I guess I had to accept given my rap sheet—and tried to make out that I had paid my mate to take the fall. I'm not quite sure how they came to that conclusion as I had spent the night in the cell and had no way of contacting him, but that's what they claimed.

I ended up being charged with vandalising both a car and the shop and appeared in court staring at a jail term. My legal advice was to plead guilty to both charges and throw myself on the mercy of the court. The magistrate gave me two choices: go to jail or leave Goulburn for a year. My solicitor and Mum had actually come up with the idea of leaving town and convinced the magistrate that it would be the best option. It probably saved me from a term behind bars. I've got to give it to the solicitor, he did a good job of selling the magistrate the merits of the move.

While I knew I would miss Mum and my family and my mates, I had already decided I was off to Atherton for the coming season. It was an easy choice—jail or leave town. Even though it was kind of embarrassing to be barred from my home town, in a way it was a blessing. It got me out of my comfort zone, out of the rut I was in, and I was able to turn my life around in steamy Far North Queensland.

I had made some bad choices in my time playing for Canberra, no doubt. I was in a dark place and at times went into self-destruct mode—I don't even know why. A lot of it was that I was young and foolish. People still ask me, 'Was it your dad's illness that was behind it all?' But I'm never going to blame it on that—it would be just making an easy excuse for my bad behaviour.

I was at my lowest while at the Canberra Raiders, and yet I feel they crucified me more than any other club. I believe the entire Canberra episode affected the rest of my career moving forward—even more so than the incident at Cronulla. The Raiders tore up my contract and cost me a year of my NRL career.

The Raiders were the club I had always dreamed of playing for but, in the end, most of my memories there are shit ones.

NEIL HENRY

The highly respected Neil Henry was coaching the Raiders in 2009 when the club made the tough call to sack Carney. For Henry, the move by the club was hard to take—but understandable. 'I liked Todd as a young bloke and also had great respect for his playing ability,' Henry says. 'The club signed him when he was around twelve and he was in the first-grade squad at seventeen, a genuine child prodigy and a special talent. Todd was popular within the group—the boys all loved him—and he was also among the first to put up his hand to do community and school work. He loved mingling with the young fellas. He was probably protected by the club for a few of his indiscretions because of his great ability and there were probably some incidents that were covered up for his own good. But after that the club put a six-point plan to him and one of the main points was that he stop drinking. Alcohol was at the root of his problems and sadly, he was one of those blokes that when they go out drinking, they just lose their moral compass and do things they would never dream of doing when they are sober.

'I think Todd and his manager underestimated the mood of the senior playing group and the board. I think they thought he would just go to another club and pick up the pieces, but [NRL boss] David Gallop stepped in and put a stop to that. I think that was really the beginning of the huge spotlight being put on player behaviour and Todd probably feels hard done by because he was made an example of. I feel for him but the bottom line is, these guys are in the spotlight, make good money and with that comes certain responsibility. Todd was young and a bit of a rebel and he just didn't quite get that.'

Henry's association with the Carney family went back to before Todd was born, in the rough-and-tumble world of bush footy in the 1980s. 'I was captain–coach of West Belconnen and we used to dread playing against Goulburn,' he recalls. 'Daryl Carney and a few of his brothers played for them and you always knew it would be a tough afternoon against the Carney boys. Daryl was a hard man and more than once he chased me around the field—and when he caught me I'd be hurting for days afterwards.

'When he had a son, I knew he would push him to be a football star and he certainly had a good one in Todd. He was among the most talented players I ever coached. He had explosive speed despite a bit of a stocky build and with that strong frame, he was able to break through tackles and get through the defensive line. He was dynamic over the first five to ten metres and that is such a valuable skill in the game these days. He was also an exceptional kicker—both for goal and in general play where he had a big boot on him. Add a smart football brain and the fact he was a good talker and you have a pretty complete footballer.

'His one weakness was that he was a little inconsistent at times and I think that was his on-field life mirroring what he was doing off the field. He was an enigma—he knew he shouldn't drink and yet he couldn't stop himself and drama inevitably followed. The guy was no dummy, though, he was quite bright and good to talk to about footy. The problem was, he never learned from his mistakes. To his credit, he would always put his hand up after the event. Some players would always find someone else to blame but with Todd, I'd call him in and ask what happened and he'd say "Yep, I did it—I'm hopeless on the drink." He knew he was a wild man with a few too many drinks in him. This was just the beginning of the social media era and players could still go out to some extent and have a good time—but things were clearly changing and he was a victim of that. He was something of a loveable rogue but really got hammered by the media and fans in general over his track record.'

Despite Carney's history of carnage, Henry attempted to sign him in 2012 after he left the Roosters. 'I was at the Cowboys and we had a few talks and he was quite keen,' Henry said. 'We sat down and had a good long talk about what he could do for us and what we could do for him. He thought getting out of Sydney would be a good move—and he was probably right. He would have found things easier in a smaller place like Townsville, away from the intense media glare of the big city. And the other big factor in our favour was that he relished the opportunity of playing alongside Johnathan Thurston— and which halfback wouldn't? They could have been a lethal combination and with his speed and 'JT's' football brain and competitiveness, it would have been great to watch them in tandem. But the Cowboys board was a bit wary of him given his track record and then in the meantime Cronulla snapped him up—so it never happened. It's a pity because I think we could have controlled him better up in that environment in North Queensland and his talent would have really added to what was already a pretty good football team.

'I think in recent years he has got more mature and realised he needed to straighten himself out, which isn't uncommon with blokes his age in all walks of life. I think he has learned some valuable life lessons and I'll be interested to see how his coaching career goes—he certainly has the football brain and charisma to be a success.'

5

ATHERTON

One of the best things I did was make the move to Far North Queensland to work in the pub at Atherton and play for the local team. It all came about when Mick Nasser, owner of the pub and president of the footy club, contacted player manager Gavin Orr looking for a guy with experience in the big league to steer the local team around the park. Gavin didn't manage me but he's a good bloke and we know each other through mates. He said to Mick, 'How about Todd Carney?' I think Mick was taken aback at first—I was pretty much public enemy number one to the media and public at that stage. Plenty of people who didn't know me could have been excused for thinking I was an axe murderer if they just followed my career through the press and television.

But Mick did his due diligence and found out I wasn't such a bad bloke after all and he invited my manager Dave Riolo up to check the place out. I'd already signed a hand-shake deal with the Roosters to go to Sydney the following year, so this was a chance to experience something different and hopefully stay out of trouble while I served my so-called de-registration from the NRL.

I liked what I saw and was immediately taken by the warmth of Mick and his wife Maree. They took me in like I was one of their kids and I lived with them at the pub. It was not long after Dad's death, so suddenly having a big family around me was just what I needed. Halfway through the year Mum moved up there and Mick gave her a job, so that was more support for me in my time of need.

As always, there were the critics. Raiders chairman John McIntyre commented to the local Canberra media that 'there must be some boofheads up there in North Queensland' to give me a job in a pub. 'That's not the environment that Todd should be in,' he added. 'It's another question of his management and whether they are making the decision in the best interest of Todd's future.' It was a flippant comment and made without any knowledge of Mick Nasser or his family and the strict conditions I was put under. There were clearly plenty of doubters in Canberra—and I was keen to try to prove them wrong.

Working 40 hours a week in a pub on top of playing football was hard yakka, but it gave me a better understanding and appreciation of the real world. You meet all sorts of people in a country pub and for a bloke with problems with alcohol, working behind the bar can be tempting. Everyone wants to be your mate and buy you a beer and the girls also showed some interest in me. But I just tried my best to keep out of strife and do the job at hand and rebuild my life and my career. It was a great experience and set the scene for probably my best year in footy the following season when I returned to the big league with the Sydney Roosters.

Some of the patrons were real characters. I remember there was this old bloke, Henry, who used to come in most nights and loved his steak dinner. But he had a few physical challenges and struggled to cut up the steak. So one day when I was working I went over quietly and cut the steak up for him. Maree Nasser cried when she saw what I was doing—apparently no one had ever done that for Henry before. I didn't think anything of it, I'd been raised to help out those less fortunate than me and while I've had my problems that everyone knows about, I like to think I have also touched a few lives in a positive way.

I did have some doubts initially about whether I'd done the right thing by going bush. The first day at training, we had about half a dozen blokes there when we were supposed to start. Others turned up in dribs and drabs, some didn't show up at all. It was country footy and no one really minded too much—so different to what I was used to in the NRL, where being even five minutes late would mean a fine and possibly a date with the reserve grade coach. I thought, 'What have I got myself into here, maybe this is one giant mistake.' But I went to bed that first night, had a long think about it, and told myself to make the most of it, to be the best I could be, be myself and see what happens—and I did.

I thought I was too young to captain–coach, which was one proposal that was put to me, so I brought a mate up from Canberra, Josh Blatch, who played reserve grade for the Raiders, and he did the job, taking a lot of the pressure off me.

The training wasn't as intense as at Canberra, obviously, and with me working in the bar, I soon started to stack on weight. They had the best crumbed schnitzels in all the east coast there and while I tried to eat healthy salads and the like, more than once I'd tell the girls in the kitchen, 'Give me a crumbed schnitzel with chips, please.'

On the field, I was obviously a target but I was still pretty young and mainly a running halfback in those days. I didn't fully understand the game like I did later in my career but I had plenty of pace and they had to catch me before they could hit me! We had a good year at Atherton and made the grand final, but lost to Cairns Brothers, which was disappointing. To come so close and lose the big one was gutting for all of us. It was a massive improvement on the previous year, though, and everyone in the club was delighted with the progress we had made.

Off the field, even in Atherton, trouble found me. One weekend my sister Krysten and her husband came up to watch me play and we went to a club for a post-match function. A couple of blokes got the shits when a girl from their group came up and chatted to me. We left because I knew this wasn't going to end well but they followed us down the street. They tried to get me to fight them but I was determined not to be baited and kept walking. Then they jumped me from behind. There must have been five or six of them. The first guy punched me straight in the eye and so my vision was shot and I struggled to defend myself. I just tried to protect my face and stay on my feet— I knew if I fell to the footpath they would have stuck the boot in and things would have got really ugly.

They eventually bolted when people started to come up and I was very lucky to get out of it with just a black eye. Police got involved and arrested four of the blokes. They were charged with assault but I didn't really want to go ahead with it. I told the cops not to bother.

I'd copped shit in Goulburn before but nothing like this—it was like a sick, pack mentality. I just wanted to put it behind me. The locals in Atherton had been great to me and from what I could gather, these guys weren't locals anyway, they were from a neighbouring town. The worst part for me was that my sister had to witness it and she was quite traumatised at the time—she had never seen anything like that before.

But that incident aside, I kept out of drama in Atherton and learned some great life lessons there as I prepared to move to the big city and back to the big league with the Roosters. I made life-long friends and got a preview on life in the real world, out of the NRL bubble which all us players find ourselves in for most of our careers.

MICK NASSER

While bush footy might have seemed a step down for the NRL star, Todd Carney looks back on his season in Atherton as a turning point not just in his career but his life. The 22-year-old's NRL career had stalled when the Canberra Raiders sacked him in the middle of 2008. Meanwhile on the Atherton Tablelands, the Atherton Roosters Senior Rugby League Club was looking around for a new captain–coach to steer the local team into grand final contention. The long-serving club president Michael Nasser, publican at the iconic heritage-listed Barron Valley Hotel, rang around several NRL managers.

'I spoke to about six of them and most didn't give me the time of day,' Mick Nasser says. 'But one bloke gave me his ear. Gavin Orr. He had a player from Cronulla who was interested, however his wife got pregnant and wanted to have their baby at home, so he pulled out at the last minute in mid-December.

'It's not a good look not having a captain–coach lined up before Christmas. Gavin lined up another bloke and he fell through. Then he said to me, "What about Todd Carney?"'

Orr was not Carney's manager, that was Dave Riolo on whose behalf he was acting. Nasser admitted he did not know much about Carney as dealing with club matters and running the family pub did not always give him the time to follow players too closely.

'He's a bit crazy, isn't he?' Nasser said to Orr. 'And he might want too much money.'

Orr stuck up for the young player. 'He's been sacked from the Raiders and we were trying to find a home for him in England,' he replied. 'Todd was offered $600,000, but it all got knocked on the head. He had two drink-driving offences and couldn't get a visa.'

Nasser thought this over and devised a package that might entice the gun five-eighth to Atherton. The Nasser family would put him up at their pub and provide him with a job while he played for the Atherton Roosters.

'I could see his worth not just for our club but for the entire Cairns District Rugby League,' Nasser says, reflecting. 'He would get supporters through the gates not just in Atherton but at all the away games around Far North Queensland.'

Before considering the sea-change to Atherton, Carney had a crack at applying to play for a team in France. Meanwhile, the Atherton Roosters still didn't have a coach. France was an illusion too because he couldn't get a visa to go there either.

'All doors are being closed to Todd. What can you do?' Orr asked Nasser.

A seasoned publican, Mick Nasser said the best thing they could do was to get Carney off the grog.

'If he has any aggression in his behaviour, I'm not interested,' he told Orr. 'Living in a hotel is not a good mix for someone with drinking problems.'

A third-generation publican, Nasser knows what he is talking about. He is no stranger to poor behaviour from intoxicated patrons. He often put up new players from out of town, which mostly worked out well.

Orr assured Nasser that Carney did not have a problem with his behaviour—especially when off the drink.

Nasser sold the Atherton Roosters committee on taking on Carney despite the 'negative stuff' in the media at the time. He told them that not many people realised that Carney's father recently died and had left him without his mentor at a young age.

'At 22, Todd has not experienced life much,' the club president told his committee. 'He cracked the NRL first grade at the age of seventeen and was on half a million dollars—that was a lot of money at his disposal.'

The farming town of Atherton is the biggest town on the southern Atherton Tablelands, a part of the Great Dividing Range. With a population of some 8000, the town is a third the size of Todd's home town of Goulburn. Crop farming and beef were thriving in 2009, but the region's famous dairy industry was collapsing. The area was formerly known as Priors Pocket or Priors Creek, named after the creek running behind the Nassers' Barron Valley Hotel in the centre of Atherton.

Nasser took over the hotel, affectionately known as the BV, in 1999. The Nasser family originally came out to Queensland from Kousba, Lebanon, in the 1890s, eventually settling in Atherton.

Mick's grandfather Alexander 'Sconder' Nasser and his wife Amelia took over ownership of the BV, then a two-storey timber hotel, in 1930. In the late 1930s, Sconder decided to replace the building with a grander and more substantial structure. Construction was completed in 1941: it had 40 bedrooms, a billiards parlour, two bars, and a lounge and dining room separated by decorative leadlight folding doors, which could be opened to create one large dance hall or ballroom. By the time Todd Carney came to town, the BV was heritage-listed and famous for its meals and cold beer and surviving with no poker machines.

Carney and Riolo flew up to Far North Queensland to check out Atherton and meet the Nassers. The day their plane was due to arrive at Cairns Airport, Mick and newly appointed captain–coach Josh Blatch headed to Cairns via the Kuranda Range Road, a section of the Kennedy Highway that runs through rainforest between Kuranda and Smithfield. Despite numerous improvements over the years, the winding mountain road was notorious for traffic accidents. And so it happened—an accident on the range prevented Mick and Josh from getting to Cairns on time.

'I didn't want the media finding out about Todd's movements so I didn't want him having to wait at the airport for any length of time,' Nasser says. 'I rang a mate and asked him to pick up Todd and his manager and we'd meet at Port Douglas.'

The Nassers turned around and hotfooted it towards Mount Molloy, where they came down to the coast via the Rex Range. They picked up Todd and drove back to Atherton.

Todd signed up the following morning and he and Riolo flew back to Sydney. He was later registered with the Queensland Rugby League.

Then another obstacle emerged before Carney could play with the Atherton Roosters. John McIntyre, the chairman of the Canberra Raiders, the team that had dumped Carney, decided he would not release him from his contract to play bush footy.

Mick and Maree were in Coogee in February 2009 to attend Maree's sister's wedding when McIntyre's 'boofhead' comment was in the media. 'I read this negative stuff about me in the national press and I wondered if it was all worth it,' Nasser says. 'We decided not to back off.

'It was on a Friday when McIntyre met with the NRL about Carney and he decided he couldn't stop him from playing for the Atherton Roosters as it was a restriction of trade and released him. It was happy days!

'On the Saturday, I went to the Randwick races and then Todd rang me while I was there and dropped a bombshell.'

'I don't think you are going to want me anymore,' Carney told Mick. 'I got locked up last night and I have a court date in six weeks.'

Carney and a mate had gone yahooing in his home town of Goulburn the night before. He had jumped on a car bonnet and his mate had damaged the entrance to a Fone Zone store. Nasser looked to the heavens and wondered what was going to happen next.

'I got on the phone to his solicitor, who told me to get a letter to him by Sunday so he could take it to a hearing with the magistrate on the Monday,' Nasser said. 'He wanted to bring Todd's court date forward so he could get up to Atherton to play the coming weekend.'

Nasser drafted a rushed letter of support for Carney on a serviette at the reception. He found the right words and wrote that he would 'father the kid' and give him a job working behind the bar at the BV.

'I wrote that Todd would learn how to deal with people, know when to cut them off,' Nasser said. 'I would teach him from the inside out about the running of a pub and a bottle shop and on three nights a week he would go to training. I would be a father figure to him and get him back on track to play in the NRL in 2010.'

The next morning Nasser had to travel to Ulladulla with family after the wedding at Coogee and with time running out went to a local newsagent to get stationery. The staff offered to type up the letter and they faxed it through to Todd's solicitor in the nick of time.

The solicitor seemed happy with the letter and took it to Monday's hearing with Todd and his mother Leanne present. The outcome was that the magistrate dropped Carney's court hearing on the vandalism charges altogether. Carney was handed a twelve-month suspended jail sentence, banned from going back to Goulburn for a year and ordered to undertake alcohol counselling.

The relieved and contrite player was grateful to get another chance and promised to sort himself out. Carney packed his bags and was bound for Far North Queensland to live in a town he had never heard of before. By the Thursday, he was in the front bar of the BV.

'As I was still in New South Wales I arranged for a friend of mine to pick him up from the Cairns airport, and I also asked him to show Todd how to pour a beer. For someone who drank a lot of beer, this was a new experience for Todd,' Nasser says.

'As soon as I arrived home later that week I laid down the law to Todd on how it was going to be while he was in Atherton for the footy season. "You put me through a world of hurt last weekend and the press gave me a hard time,"' he told his new young charge. '"Let's make this a win–win. If you get to make a new start in the NRL, it will be a feel-good story for us. If you get into trouble, you will lose your career and it's curtains for you. The media will have a field day with me, but I don't care, it will blow over in a couple of months. So this is what's going to happen. You are here to work and to get your shit sorted. You can drink within the four walls of this hotel, but no going out anywhere else. I can't babysit you, but you are banned from going to Cairns except to play football. You will only leave Atherton if you come with us. You won't go anywhere without us watching you."'

Todd agreed and got the keys to Room 28 upstairs, a little en suite room with a small balcony on the right wing of the BV. (After Carney left Atherton, guests who were league fans often asked if they could stay in the 'Todd Carney Suite'.)

He found working full-time in the pub on top of playing football to be hard work, especially under the strict conditions Mick Nasser laid down. The Nassers and fellow staff kept a close watch over him. Carney felt the BV gave him a better understanding and appreciation of the real world.

With his Responsible Service of Alcohol qualifications under his belt, Todd had a baptism of fire on his first Friday night. He was working the front bar and noticed one man had fallen asleep at the bar and another intoxicated man was getting rest-less. Todd asked Mick how to handle the situation. Mick advised him to stand in front of the sleeper, not behind him and shake him awake. Too often sleeping patrons wake up surprised and punch the person behind them. When Todd asked the other bloke to leave, the drunk threatened to cut his throat. He once admitted to Maree that working at the BV had given him an appreciation of the behaviour of people on the drinking side of the bar. 'I can see how silly I've been from the other side of the bar,' he said.

Nasser says the young women found Carney to be a charming lad with a quiet personality. 'A lot of girls flirted with the new boy in town and tried to hit on him.' He was proud of how Carney conducted himself and turned his life around while working at the pub and playing football.

On the field, Carney impressed. After he played a few games people could see he had talent. 'He addressed his critics,' Nasser says.

At his first game against Cairns Suburbs, about 2500 people went through the gates to see Carney play. Suburbs targeted the former NRL star and Carney copped some nasty head-high tackles and one where his jaw almost snapped. He told Nasser after the match that he had not been hit around the head so much before. Nasser bailed up the referee and suggested he keep a closer eye out in future matches for blatant head-high and rough play against Carney. 'We won that match and we won every match up until the grand final,' Mick says.

Club stalwart Jamie Blain held the fort while the club looked around for a new coach and eventually appointed Josh Blatch as captain–coach. Formerly a lower grade player and coach with the Canberra Raiders, Blatch knew Carney and agreed to come up. Carney's signing had attracted several local boys wanting to play with the Atherton Roosters.

While Carney's drinking was curbed, he was allowed to knock back a few with his teammates after a game. One night, however, he got Mick's reluctant permission to have a few beers at another venue in Atherton's Main Street with his sister Krysten, who was visiting with her husband to watch Todd play. Mick didn't want him to go out. 'I was nervous about it, but his friends promised me they would look after him.'

Nasser's worst feelings were realised when six youths ambushed Carney in the street, beating and kicking him.

After the commotion, Mick went to check on Todd and he was in his room packing his bags.

'I've had enough. I want to go home,' Todd said.

'What did I say about going out?' Mick said. 'You've just got to ride this out, Todd. Besides, you can't go home, you're banned from Goulburn.'

Mick went to the police and they checked the closed-circuit television footage, which clearly showed that Todd had been set upon without provocation.

On another occasion, Todd was keen to join his Atherton Roosters' mates at the Mount Garnet races. Nasser was not keen, especially as he and Maree were going to Brisbane that weekend while there was a bye.

'Mate, you can't go to Mount Garnet,' Nasser told him. 'It's the last place for you to go. You'll be fodder. If you want to go out, come with Maree and me to Brisbane.'

Todd went to Sydney to see his sister and then flew to Brisbane to spend time with Mick and Maree. They also visited Maree's home town of Gatton to see family. Carney behaved like a gentleman the entire weekend.

The Atherton Roosters signed up Sydney player Gray Viane later in the season, but Nasser felt he was leading Todd astray and discouraged the friendship. Viane constantly tried to cajole Todd into joining him for a beer and going up the road. But the Nassers were vigilant. And on another occasion, Maree stayed in the bar especially to keep an eye on Todd as a couple of lads from Mareeba were trying to get Todd out to the nightclub scene in Cairns. One of them leant over the bar and said to the bar attendant, Mick and Maree's then twenty-year-old daughter Regina: 'Tell your mother to fuck off!' Regina was shocked.

Unimpressed with Viane, who he believed had seen better days on the paddock, Mick eventually showed him the door.

'Jack Gibson used to say if you want to get rid of someone, give them an apple and a map. So that's what I gave Viane.'

Not being allowed home, Todd missed his family during his Atherton year. His mother Leanne came up to visit and the Nassers offered her an en suite room and job in the BV bottle shop up the road and she cleaned rooms at the BV. Leanne stayed for six months and was a rock of Gibraltar for her 22-year-old son. Todd's sister Melinda visited a couple times too, helping to keep Todd grounded, even though she had a similar personality to Todd.

As the season came to a close, the Atherton Roosters had won the minor premiership and were looking good for the grand final at Barlow Park in Cairns. That's where all Cairns District Rugby League (CDRL) grand finals were played. The Roosters went into the grand final with two injured front-rowers and an injured coach. They were up against their arch rivals, Cairns Brothers. Brothers scored two freakish tries, with one rebounding off the goalposts, and easily converted them to make the score 12–0 in the first five minutes. Roosters got to the lead at half-time. 'But Todd's kicking shoes weren't on,' Mick Nasser says. It wasn't the Atherton Roosters' year.

All the same, CDRL was rubbing its hands, delighted to get 8000 people turning out for the big match. CDRL grand finals average an attendance of 3000–4000. Carney, the main attraction of the 2009 CDRL season, made a lot of money for the Atherton club and the CDRL.

The Sydney Roosters were keen to formally sign Carney and kept tabs on him while he was in Atherton. They kept in touch with Nasser for updates on his behaviour.

Todd ended the year on a high, having been named the Atherton club's Player of the Year at the presentations.

'It was a sad day when Todd left town,' Mick reminisces. 'We put him on a plane to Brisbane with his career with the NRL back on track. The consensus was he wouldn't make it. But he was in form with the Sydney Roosters and had lost none of his speed and skills. It was a proud moment for us when he was named Man of the Match after his first NRL game with the Sydney Roosters, which we attended with Todd's family. In fact, early in the pre-season in February 2010, a punter at the BV suggested I put a bet on Carney winning the Dally M. I thought why not? It was paying $51, so I put $120 on him. I told a few other blokes and they put something on.'

Nasser got on to Todd and said: 'Do yourself a favour and stay off the grog the whole of this year and see how you go. He told me he had already decided to do that. He had learned in Atherton he didn't need to rely on the grog.'

As the season progressed, Carney was clearly the stand-out player of the year and the odds shortened for the Dally M. The Sydney Roosters, in appreciation of the Nassers' success in rehabilitating their star player, flew Mick down for the Dally M Awards. It was an opportunity to catch up with Todd's mum Leanne, who had worked at the BV the previous year. 'When Todd's name was announced, we were thrilled, it was great,' Nasser said.

A keen punter, Nasser was delighted to win $6120 on his bet. He and Todd and a few other blokes bought shares in a racehorse. 'He won five or so races,' Nasser says.

The Roosters went on to the grand final and the Nassers went down for the big one, but, sadly, Sydney Roosters, like their Atherton counterparts the year before, missed out.

In 2014 the Nassers and Leanne Carney scored corporate seats when Cronulla played Brisbane Broncos. The Broncos were leading comfortably and someone passed comments about Carney not featuring in play. Nasser warned the patron, '"I wouldn't say too much as his mum is in earshot . . . she will give you hell." In the second half, Todd put Brisbane to the sword. He single-handedly destroyed the Broncos with a couple of tries and set up a few more. He was Man of the Match and it was happy days again. Little did we know it would not last.'

Within 48 hours, Nasser's phone was running hot following the infamous 'bubbler' photo.

'My son, who was also at that game, rang me a day or so later and asked me if I had heard about Todd and he told me about the bubbler photo,' Nasser says. 'Every time the press got something on Todd, they would ring me and they certainly hounded me over that incident—but as with previous incidents, I was 100 per cent behind him. He has made some poor decisions on the drink but he is a lovely person and we liked him so much we invited him back to captain–coach Atherton in the club's centenary year in 2018. Sadly for us he had already committed to play for the Northern Pride, but he is still welcome back any time. He is family to us and our town.'

6

ROOSTERS

Being a country lad, I'd never lived in Sydney before and it was a bit intimidating as a newcomer. But I soon learned the ropes and where to go and not to go—even though I, of course, lapsed occasionally and fell to temptation.

I signed with Sydney Roosters while up in Atherton. Nick Politis was prepared to give me a go and I am eternally grateful to him. It was a good career move, joining such a professional club under a top-notch coach in Brian Smith, who was signed after I had agreed terms. Looking at my career, I would say that the making of me was in Canberra but I really came of age at the Roosters in 2010.

My time at the Roosters didn't start in ideal fashion—overdoing it on the drink got me in the shit again. It was New Year's Eve 2010 and me and a few of my mates from Goulburn went on a boys' trip to Airlie Beach in the Whitsundays.

There were about half a dozen of us sharing a big apartment and it was a typical boozy boys' trip with the 'rules' that young blokes put in place for these type of holidays. There are 'penalties'—like the first bloke to quit drinking and go to bed can expect to wake up with an eyebrow missing or a new haircut. It's silly, it's juvenile, but it's fun at the time and usually harmless. But on this particular occasion, a mate of mine, Brad Smith, was the unfortunate one to hit the sack before anyone else. I've known Brad all my life—his dad, Bob, was my cricket coach when I was a kid—and he is a great fella.

In my intoxicated state I decided to take our 'game' one step further. I took a cigarette lighter and a can of deodorant and snuck into the bedroom, where he was in a deep sleep. I sprayed the deodorant at his backside and lit it with the lighter, my aim being to scare the hell out of him and give him a sore bum for a second. I bolted out of the room and slammed the door but, unbeknown to me in my drunken state, I did too good a job and started a little fire in the bed!

A couple of minutes later, Brad came flying out of the room—smoke coming from his arse—and naturally enough he wasn't happy. I was genuinely shocked—just another example of being stupid on the piss back-firing on me big time. There were burns to the backs of his legs and we took him to a medical centre, where they gave him some cream and said he would be alright, but it was a nasty burn and hurt him a fair bit. Brad was okay with it though and we all stayed up there three or four more nights before heading home. It wasn't a major fight or anything like that, even though I felt awful at the pain I had caused him. I thought that was the end of it but someone saw me and him at the medical centre and next thing I knew the media were onto it, there were cameras everywhere. I was front page news again and the Roosters, who I still hadn't played a game for, were not happy—and understandably so.

Thankfully, that scandal died down after a couple of days and I was able to resume my new life as a Rooster. The club—and the metropolis of Sydney—were very different to the lifestyle I was used to in Canberra and Goulburn. The Raiders were a really laidback club and Canberra was pretty much a big country town—we'd hit the shops in thongs and singlets after training without a second thought. The Roosters had a reputation of being suave, latte-sipping blokes—and I didn't even drink coffee! I had no idea what a sushi train was until I moved to Sydney's east. But I did notice that when we went out, the dress standards were a bit higher and it took some getting used to for a boy from the bush.

I lived with Phil Graham, another former Raider, in Maroubra. It was close to the beach but being a Goulburn boy, I wasn't a surfie or anything like that and didn't have much to do with the sand and sea.

I got a shock at my very first training session when Brian Smith told me, 'I'm moving you to fullback.' It came out of the blue and my first thought was how Anthony Minichiello would react to the news. 'Mini' was a club legend and one of the best fullbacks in the game and I would have understood if he'd been kicking stones and looking at me like I was a grub for taking his spot. But he was a champion about it and his attitude was that if 'Smithy' wanted me at fullback and him on the wing and it was best for the team, so be it. He even went to the extent of giving me tips on fullback play, and I will be forever grateful to him for that. I'd never really played the position for any length of time and felt all at sea at the beginning. At around 95 kilograms I was bigger than normal from my stint in Atherton—probably four or five kilos heavier than usual—from not training full-time and living in the pub. I could see where Smithy was coming from with the move—he probably thought I was too big to play in the halves at the elite level.

The thing I dreaded most about switching to fullback was the prospect of defusing bombs. I'm not the biggest bloke, and that automatically put me at a disadvantage when I had these giant wingers and back-rowers trying to beat me to the ball in the air. I reckon I lost sleep those first few weeks after Smithy switched me, thinking about the high, spiral bomb in the air and half the opposition team bearing down on me. I used to dread whenever the team we were playing got over halfway with the ball because I knew that meant one thing—the bomb was about to head my way on the sixth tackle and the hordes were coming to get me. Rival coaches knew that I was new to fullback and would probably be nervous—and they were right! I reckon I had my eyes closed sometimes when I went up for the ball. I just jumped and prayed.

Fortunately my wingers dropped back to help take some of the pressure off me and it wasn't as bad as I thought. As it was, I handled fullback okay in the early rounds and then ended up moving back into the halves during State of Origin when Mitchell Pearce was playing for New South Wales. Then, after Origin, Smithy moved Braith Anasta to the edge, Mini got his number one jumper again and I was back in the halves full-time with 'Pearcey', and I must admit I felt happier and more comfortable there.

•

Appropriately, my Sydney Roosters career formally begun in Atherton, where I made so many friends the previous year and was able to get my career back on track. It was the Roosters' way of saying 'thank you' to the town for taking me in and it was great to have my first hit-out in the red, white and blue up there. It felt strange wearing these new colours against the locals, but they gave me a good reception. It was my first game at fullback and I did well in a big confidence booster for what lay ahead.

The next game, I had a bigger test in the annual Foundation Cup against the Tigers. I made a good impact, enjoying chiming into the back line, and I formed a good combination with Mitchell Pearce. Mitch and I had plenty in common—we both had our share of drama on the drink—and we became great mates off the field and a good pairing on it.

A few weeks later, we played the season opener—and it was against the Roosters' old rivals South Sydney. Growing up in Goulburn, this game never meant much to me but as soon as I moved to Maroubra—near the border of Souths' and Roosters' territory—I quickly realised what a massive thing it is. Everyone in the area supports either the Roosters or Rabbitohs, and they can't wait for this game between Australian rugby league's two oldest rivals—it's all they want to talk about. It's almost like the Fibros (Wests) versus Silvertails (Manly) class wars that Roy Masters made famous in the 1970s—the battlers from Souths against the upper-class Roosters. And it seemed that whichever team won the game went on to have a strong season, while the loser usually struggled to recover. For years Souths against Roosters kicked off the season and was played with the intensity of a finals game before a massive crowd, though for some reason in recent years the scheduling has changed, which is a pity for the fans who waited for it so eagerly. I was glad to see the NRL brought it back to the first round in 2019, when Souths ambushed the Roosters—the reigning premiers—in a major upset.

I knew Souths would test me out, being a rookie in the fullback spot at a new club, making my comeback to the NRL after a year away—and test me out they did. Fortunately, it was one of those games where we were on the front foot from the outset and things went our way, and they didn't enjoy enough field position to make my life difficult. I stood up to everything Souths threw at me and had a big game in attack, making a few long breaks with the extra room I had to move at fullback.

The highlight for me was chasing a kick—I think by Braith Anasta—that looked like being too long. Just before it reached the dead ball line, I swatted it back into play and Sammy Perrett scored. In a game that usually went down to the wire, we showed our potential for a strong year by smashing the Bunnies 36–10, the biggest margin between the teams for some time.

I got Man of the Match—another great thing for my confidence on the long road ahead. But most pleasing for me was that my mum and sisters—and Mick and Maree Nasser, who had become part of my family during my time in Atherton—were there to watch me. The club flew Mick and Maree down to Sydney as a show of thanks for looking after me for that year when I was out of the NRL and keeping me on the road to redemption. I kept up my good form in the opening month or so of the season, but it was pretty easy as I had good players around me and we were winning more than losing.

I came to the Roosters with a 'new kid on the block' mentality, feeling I had a point to prove, especially after how badly things ended at Canberra and the fact I had been out of the game for a year. It was a squad brimming with talent and experience and Smithy had us playing some good football. I was loving the change and enjoying being in the headlines for the right reasons. But football can be a cruel game sometimes and you can come back to earth very quickly.

In Round 2 we had another big win—this time over the Tigers—before we had an absolute shocker in Round 3, leaking 60 points against a red-hot Bulldogs side. I'd never been thumped by so many points in my life and I found it dead-set embarrassing. I really felt for our fans who had to sit through it. We were trying . . . but everything they touched turned to gold while we just fell apart.

There was a lot of soul-searching that week, especially as we had a short turnaround of five days before a real test against a big-name Broncos side. In front of our own fans at the Sydney Football Stadium we put the pride back in the jumper with a very satisfying 25–6 win. The forwards got on top early and gave me plenty of room to move and I made the most of it. I scored two tries, landed four goals and added a field goal to score seventeen of our points. I was starting to feel very much at home in the red white and blue.

Two weeks later in Round 6 we had an early match-up with Canberra, and of course the media loved making headlines out of the 'Carney to face the club that sacked him' story in the week leading up to the game. I did feel a little extra pressure coming into the match, knowing all eyes would be on me, but it was one of those nights where everything went right for me. We played well as a team, winning 36–6, and I scored sixteen points and was again named Man of the Match. There was no gloating though, I had mates in the Canberra side and felt for them; although they left their mark on me in the form of a couple of broken ribs from a heavy hit midway through the match.

I decided to play on with the injury the following week, and had a shocker in another of the year's really big games—the traditional ANZAC Day clash at Allianz Stadium against the Dragons. I didn't take any time off when I broke my ribs and, in retrospect, should probably have taken a break. But I'd been playing well and didn't want to halt my momentum. The pain was pretty intense at times for the next four weeks or so, and it affected my confidence and ability to run the ball, and my form suffered as a result.

Smithy could see I had lost that spark and before the Round 14 clash with the Storm he said to me, 'I think it's time we moved you back into the halves.' Braith shifted to lock, a position he handled well, and I revelled at being closer to the play again. I didn't mind fullback, but always considered myself a halfback or five-eighth.

I have to credit Smithy. I feel that playing at fullback made me a better five-eighth in the long run—it really improved my running game and gave me a different perspective on things that I was able to use to my advantage.

Around that time, the *Daily Telegraph* ran a story saying I only had to keep up my good form to win selection in the Kangaroos for the Four Nations at the end of the season. I had mixed feelings when I read it—playing for Australia would have been the ultimate and it was great to know the Test selectors were looking seriously at me. But at the same time, it put pressure on me coming into the finals. I knew there was more at stake than just winning or losing every week and one bad game could blow my chances of playing for my country.

The Roosters had a couple of stutters in the second half of the season—including three straight losses—but finished the regular season strongly with wins over the Sea Eagles and Cowboys. The resurgent Dragons under Wayne Bennett won the minor premiership but we were well in the hunt for the title, coming into the finals in sixth spot but with only three fewer wins than the Dragons. I had the goal-kicking duties and was happy with the way I was striking them, bagging over 200 points and finishing second top scorer in the league.

It is during the week leading into the finals that one of the league year's biggest events is held—Dally M night. The annual awards night has developed into one of the highlights of the rugby league calendar, and all through the second half of the 2010 comp, after the voting went behind closed doors, there was plenty of talk that I was going to win it. I tried to block it out before games. If you think about stuff like that you just put additional pressure on your shoulders, but on the night I remember thinking, 'I might actually do this.'

Jake Friend was my chauffeur—he was also my flatmate and another bloke who'd had plenty of ups and downs in his career, so it was appropriate we went together. I also took Mum as my 'date' for the night, as a way of thanking her for always being there for me, through thick and thin. I don't think many players could make it to the top without the support of their mums early in their careers. Mums are the unsung heroes, the ones who cook our food, drive us to games, provide emotional support and never ask anything in return. I think Mum knew from pretty early on that I wasn't going to be a rocket scientist, so footy was my best chance of making a decent living for myself, and she went the extra mile to help me get there.

The awards were held at one of the flashiest venues in Sydney—the historic State Theatre on Market Street—and I remember having plenty of butterflies as we drove into town. The night itself was all a bit of a blur. I remember the votes going down to the wire and the counting being so very close. Right till the death, I had no idea I was going to win, although, looking back, there were a few clues. I was just too dazed by the bright lights at the time to figure them out.

One clue was the cameras all around me as the final votes were getting counted, and journalists asking me, 'So how long is your mum staying with you here in Sydney? When is she going home?' I told them that she was down for a couple of days but I wondered, 'Why are you asking me questions like that?'

In the end, I polled 27 points, one ahead of Robbie Farah of the Tigers and two in front of Darius Boyd of the Broncos. The crowd erupted when my name was announced and Mum and Smithy both gave me warm hugs. Everyone wanted to shake my hand and slap me on the back—it was a surreal feeling. I have no idea what I said when I got up on stage—the bright lights, the camera flashes, the realisation of what had just happened was all too much for me to take in. I just hope I didn't say anything idiotic because I was a blithering mess.

Just to cap a perfect night, I also won the Provan-Summons Medal—the People's Choice Award for player of the season, voted for by the fans. That meant as much to me as the Dally M Medal itself. I'd copped plenty of flak from some fickle fans over the years so to get the award was a real surprise and I can't thank the supporters enough.

But while it was a great reward for me, at the end of the day the people I really needed to thank were Nick Politis for having faith in signing me, and my teammates at the Roosters—they were the ones who had enabled me to play the best footy of my career and get the accolades. Guys like Mitchell Pearce, Shaun Kenny-Dowall and Jared Waerea-Hargreaves were playing out of their skins and they took my game to the next level.

We had a big game against the Tigers a few days later, so I stayed on the lemonade and we had an early night. But I do remember waking up the next morning and saying to Mum, 'Did that *really* happen last night?' That's how shocked I was by the whole thing. Even now, when I think back to it all, it blows me away—that I could beat so many brilliant players to take out the game's biggest award—and that the fans also rallied to pick me as their number one.

When I go home to Mum's in Goulburn, I sometimes sneak a peek at the medals and the photos of that night— it makes me smile. I don't rate it as a career highlight. I rate the whole 2010 season and how far I came after being at rock bottom a year earlier, but it was certainly right up there.

Next morning I appeared live on the *Today* show on Channel 9 and was still a bit of a stunned mullet, tired and shocked and coming to terms with it all. I just nodded and said 'yep' to most of the questions they asked me, but I think everyone could tell how happy, and a little shocked, I was.

The awards made it a bit hard to focus on the upcoming finals, but I knew I had to get my head screwed back on in a hurry so I tried to push it all into the background and concentrate on the team and the game plan.

In the opening round of the big end-of-season matches, we played what has been described as one of the greatest finals games of the modern era against the Tigers, who had come third in the regular season and had plenty of strike power.

I remember I felt tired and mentally exhausted as I ran onto the field that night. I'd never been through a week like that, with all the emotion and media focus, and it took its toll on me. I guess the great players get used to handling those situations—dealing with the adoring fans and media and then going into game mode at training and on the field—but for me, it was all very new and hard to juggle.

We started the game poorly and were down 15–2 early in the second half and looking at an early end to our year. But the big Tigers forwards started to get tired and I got room to move as the game opened up, and I put both Braith and Pearcey over for tries: suddenly it was 15–14 with less than ten minutes on the clock. There was a famous incident when Tigers forward Simon Dwyer smashed our prop Jared Waerea-Hargreaves with less than two minutes left. These days it would have been a penalty—even though it was a great shot—but the referee ruled Jared had lost the ball and it was a scrum feed to the Tigers.

My heart sank—the game was done—they just had to hang on to the ball and time would run out. The Tigers actually won the scrum but failed to pick up the rolling ball. One of our guys pounced on it and suddenly we had a pulse again. We were deep on the attack in the final minute but the Tigers' defence hung on grimly. In desperation, in the last play of the game, Braith snapped a great pressure field goal to tie the game at 15–all. This sent the game into extra time—the first final to go that way since golden point was introduced in 2003.

Both sides were exhausted, but we felt we had the momentum and confidence on our side. The Tigers knew they had blown a massive opportunity and that had to be messing with their heads.

The first five minutes of golden point were scoreless as the tension built in front of a big crowd at Allianz. I had a shot at field goal and missed—ditto Pearcey, and Robbie Farah for the Tigers. Finally, Shaun Kenny-Dowall pounced on a loose pass from Tigers forward Liam Fulton and set sail for the tryline. He went from one side of the field to the other with half the Tigers team in hot pursuit. He got the ball 60 metres out but I reckon he ran about 80 metres—it seemed to take forever but he got there and the game was ours 19–15. We were ecstatic.

I had to feel for the Tigers. I've lost a few golden point games in my time and it really is a kick in the guts. And for that to happen in a finals game only makes it worse. It was a little bit of a consolation for them that it was a try that beat them and not a flukey field goal.

I think I prefer the idea of golden try to golden point. At the moment we see too many games develop into mad scrambles for a field goal and teams not even trying to score tries in extra time—just working the ball downfield with five quick play-the-balls and then taking a shot for the point. The field goal was always one of the strengths of my game and I spent a lot of time trying to perfect it, because it can be the difference between winning and losing a tight game. But golden try is a more positive approach and I believe it would really test players and see who can rise to the occasion under that intense pressure, and make a better spectacle for the fans.

Our tails were up after that gutsy win over the Tigers, and the following week we smashed Penrith 34–12. We were always in command and the game meant a lot to several of the club's veteran players. It was the first time we had met the Panthers in the finals since the 2003 grand final, when Penrith scored a shock win. While it will never make up for the disappointment of that night, our older guys saw it as 'payback time' and took a lot of delight at sending the Panthers packing and moving a step closer to the grand final.

We were on a roll and there was no stopping us now. In the preliminary final we steamrolled the Titans 32–6. A grand final spot was ours!

It felt like we had climbed to the top of the mountain, but we knew we would be facing a formidable task against a rejuvenated Dragons side that was finally reaching its potential under the master coach Wayne Bennett.

•

Grand final week was a whirlwind and something of a circus. I would have loved more time to actually train and concentrate on the game but we had so many media and sponsor and fan commitments it wasn't possible. Having said that, I'm not complaining—it was the same for both teams and a wonderful experience to be a part of.

I found I was the centre of a lot of the media attention because of my roller-coaster journey, and that placed a fair bit of pressure on my shoulders. The media loved making a big deal of my story—the kid sacked by Canberra has a year out of the big league, goes bush, works in a pub, joins the Roosters, helps them to the grand final in his first year and wins the Dally M to boot. It generated plenty of headlines. At least they were positive for a change, but I would have preferred a little less attention.

The day after the Dallies, my manager Dave Riolo said to me, 'You do realise you are now the new face of the game?' It suddenly hit me that my life had been changed by the award. I was front and back page news for good things and everyone in the game loved my redemption story.

But I wasn't ready for the title of 'face of the game' and wasn't comfortable with it at all. I still had my demons to conquer. Alcohol was still a problem and I often resorted to it when things got tough or Dad's absence got to me. I was still an immature kid from the bush in a lot of ways. I loved being the winner of the Dally M, but I didn't want that new-found responsibility on my shoulders. To me it was just extra pressure on a kid who at times struggled with the fame that rugby league placed on him.

Leading up to the big one, I was surprised at the fact that I wasn't too nervous—I had a lot of belief in myself and my teammates. We had played well all year and knew if we were at our best, we would give it a hell of a shake.

All week, I thought of my dad and how much it would have meant to him to see me in the biggest game of the year.

When I went to the game, in my kit bag was a locket on a chain containing some of his ashes. It was just my way of having him with me in spirit on this big day. I knew Dad was watching over me and hopefully would help guide me to a good game and my destiny. I'd worn the same locket to the Dally Ms a few weeks earlier for luck. Me and my two sisters and Mum have all got one that we take around with us to remind us of Dad and the huge influence he played in our lives—and to remind us he is always there with us. Dad and I dreamed that I would win a grand final one day for Canberra. That never happened, but I saw this grand final as a second chance to realise his dream.

The big night finally came around and I can say that running out there at Homebush on that massive arena before 80,000 fans was probably the most memorable moment of my career. I've played Origin and Test football, but going out to battle for the premiership with sixteen guys who you have worked so hard with all season is as good as it gets. Just thinking about it now, it still gives me goosebumps almost ten years later.

Sadly, after the high of running out and standing arm-in-arm as they played the national anthem, it all went downhill for us. It was one of those games where the bounce of the ball and the referee's decisions just didn't go our way the whole night. We had two tries disallowed in the first half and that really took the wind out of our sails.

We held a narrow 8–6 lead at the break but going into half-time, I didn't feel comfortable and neither did the rest of the boys—we knew it should have been a greater lead. Come the second half and the Dragons put on a typical Wayne Bennett team performance. They basically strangled the life out of us.

The Dragons kept it simple, gave us nothing, waited for us to make some mistakes, and then pounced. Jamie Soward's kicking game was spot on and early in the second half he forced a line drop-out. In the following set, winger Jason Nightingale scored—our lead was gone and we never got it back. The rest of the game was pretty much a nightmare as we were camped deep in our own territory, attempting to deflect wave after wave of attack. Our spirit was eventually broken and between the 60th and 70th minutes they ran in four tries and the scoreline finished at an embarrassing 32–8.

It was a huge disappointment, but I still look back on the year with a great deal of pride—we got to a grand final and fourteen other teams wished they could have said that. Ironically, though they are light years apart on the football landscape, my 2009 year with Atherton and 2010 with Sydney Roosters were very similar. The two clubs had miserable seasons the year before, then did great to make the grand final—only to fall agonisingly short.

For me personally, it was probably my best year and I have no doubt why that was. Early on in the season I resolved to stay off the drink, which for me was no easy thing. Two other guys who have had their issues on the piss over the years—Jake Friend and Nate Myles—joined me in abstaining, and we got each other through a long, hard season, encouraging each other when we needed a boost.

That was a valuable lesson learned: you stay off the drink, good things happen, on and off the field.

But, sadly, that lesson wouldn't stick with me over the next few years.

JAKE FRIEND

When Todd Carney joined the Roosters and moved in with Jake Friend in May 2010, critics dubbed the club 'The Betty Ford clinic of rugby league'. Both had had repeated incidents with alcohol over the years and on the face of it, the pairing of two problem children seemed a disaster waiting to happen. But the duo immediately struck a pact to stay off the drink for the entire season and were instrumental in leading the Roosters to the grand final after the club had finished in last spot the previous year.

'Toddy and I both knew we were at the crossroads,' Friend recalls. 'The Roosters sacked me in 2009 after I'd made some stupid decisions on the drink and I went out and got a real job for several months in a fast food shop before they gave me a second chance. Todd was in the same boat after the Raiders tore up his contract and he spent the year up in Atherton working in the pub and playing for his local team. So it was good timing for both of us. We discovered that you could have fun without getting blind on alcohol, just by enjoying each other's company and hanging out with mates.

'It made it easier that we did it together. I'm not sure I could have stayed off the drink for so long alone but with the two of us supporting each other, it worked out well. We were committed to repaying the Roosters and Nick Politis for having faith in us—they could easily have brushed us both. We went on the paleo diet and we did a lot of extra training, just the two of us. We were both coming back into the NRL after an enforced break and knew it would take a lot of extra effort to get back up to speed. Todd had been through it all and I'd had my fair share of drama so we shared our stories about our mistakes and tried to convince each other not to make them again.

'We had similar backgrounds. We were both country boys and had both been living with other families who had taken us in—him up north and me with a nice family in the east—before deciding to pair up. I needed that family environment to settle me down after some hard times but was ready to branch out now and Todd was the perfect partner. He was funny, easy-going, and very driven—I think he got that from his dad. He was determined to make up for lost time and was really focused on having a big year in his return to the NRL.

'We had a good lifestyle. We trained hard but then, living near the beach, would go for a swim in the afternoon and then took turns cooking dinner. I reckon I was the better cook—but if you ask him he would probably say the opposite! We were both single at that stage and would spend most nights just chilling on the couch watching TV or talking. It wasn't the most exciting lifestyle for two young bachelors, but we wanted no distractions and no trouble—we were men with a mission. We both grew up some fending for ourselves, and appreciated the Roosters giving us that trust to do the right thing.'

Friend is better qualified than most to comment on the public image of Carney as opposed to the real thing. 'People would say to me that I was living with a raving lunatic,' Friend says. 'And yes, Todd did have a wild side when he had too much to drink, but when we were together and off the piss, he was quiet, polite, shy and a real good mentor and role model to young kids, although he never sought publicity for that, so few people knew about his work with young blokes behind the scenes.'

When Carney won the Dally M Medal late in that memorable season of 2010, Friend was chauffeur on the night. 'I reckon I was as happy as Toddy when they announced he had won the medal,' Friend says. 'I know how hard he had worked for it and how tough his battle was. Living with him, I got to see first-hand the sacrifices he made and the determination he had to prove the critics wrong—and there were plenty of them. His drive and success were an inspiration to me and a big reason why my career got back on the rails after my problems. He showed me it could be done and I am forever grateful. His triumph was just a great thing to witness and a part of my life I will never forget.'

Even at age one, I loved having a ball in my hand!

Running around against bigger kids in my first season at age four—Mum would often have to bribe me with sweets to play.

By under 8s, I was enjoying the game and we had a pretty strong side at North Goulburn with my dad coaching us. I am middle row, far right.

A great family moment: winning the Steve Roach Cup with my mum, Leanne, and dad, Daryl, as part of 'team Carney'.

At Seiffert Oval, 2002, aged sixteen, with my Man of the Match award after winning the under 18 grand final with Goulburn Stockmen against Queanbeyan 21–20.

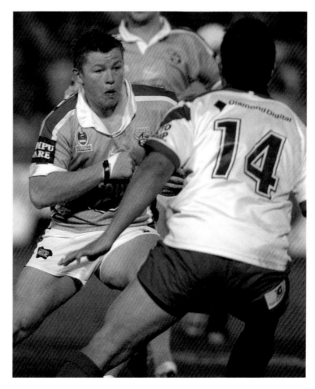

Facing off against the Bulldogs' Reni Maitua in my first game in the NRL in 2004. What a daunting night that was! (NRL Imagery)

At my 21st birthday party in Goulburn with Dad, Krysten, Mum and Melinda.

Kicking for the Raiders—the club I had followed since I was three—early in my career in 2007. *(Ian Hitchock/Getty Images)*

Touchdown! Scoring for the Green Machine against the Warriors in 2007. *(Mark Nolan/Getty Images)*

Helping the locals rebuild their lives in Rwanda in 2008. What a life-altering experience that was for me. *(Gregg Porteous/Newspix)*

Todd Payten, Nathan Hindmarsh, me and Justin Poore hanging out with the locals during a visit to Sonrise Primary School in Rwanda. The kids knew nothing about rugby league but loved sharing stories with us. *(Gregg Porteous/Newspix)*

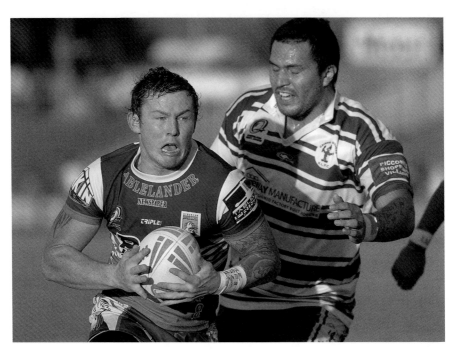

Playing for Atherton Roosters during my year 'in exile' in 2009. I learnt a lot about life that year. *(Michael Watt/Newspix)*

A funny moment: my first game for the Sydney Roosters against my former club the Raiders—the fans gave it to me!

One of the high points: winning the Dally M in 2010, with mum. I was so glad I could make her proud. (Gregg Porteous/ Newspix)

Mitchell Pearce and I had a special chemistry, on and off the field. Here we celebrate our big win over Penrith in the 2010 finals at Allianz Stadium. *(NRL Imagery)*

Fending off Mark Gasnier of the Dragons in the 2010 grand final. Sadly it wasn't to be our night. *(Phil Hillyard/Newspix)*

My one and only match for Australia was against the Kiwis in 2010. It's a game I will always treasure. *(Hannah Peters/Getty Images)*

Legendary coach Warren Ryan congratulating me on winning International Player of the Year in 2010, another great moment. *(NRL Imagery)*

Playing for Country against City in 2012—a stepping stone to my State of Origin debut. *(Mark Kolbe/Getty Images)*

Still coming to terms with my selection for New South Wales at the Blues' first media call in 2012.

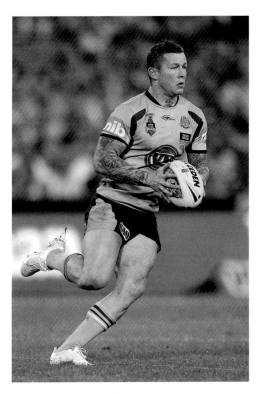

State of Origin game two, 2012.
I found Origin was everything
they said it would be.
(Cameron Spencer/Getty Images)

Kicking for goal was a job I enjoyed—and I spent many hours practising the art.
The multi-coloured socks I wore in this game against the Bulldogs in 2011 were
to raise money to fight dementia. *(Ryan Pierse/Getty Images)*

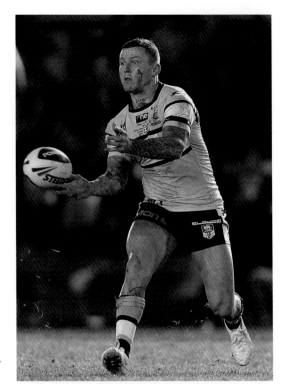

Bleeding for the Sharks
against Manly in 2014.
I thought I played my most
consistent football at Cronulla.
(Renee McKay/Getty Images)

My last game for the Sharks in
2014, coming from behind to
beat the Broncos in Brisbane.
(Bradley Kanaris/Getty Images)

Keeping the ball moving for Catalans against Wakefield in 2016. I had some great experiences travelling around Europe while I played there. *(Nigel Roddis/ Getty Images)*

With my great mate Boyd Cordner in Bali. We often hang out together in our down time.

I've never been a fighter, but I did enjoy my one and only bout against cheeky Chris Sandow, which ended in a draw. *(Christopher Pearce/Fairfax)*

On the run for Salford Red Devils against Catalans in 2017. We had some good wins and a lot of fun off the field. *(Alexandre Dimou/Icon Sport)*

Playing in my final stint in the big league, for Hull KR. Injuries restricted my game time there. *(HDM)*

Playing against Ballina as captain–coach of Byron Bay in Round 8 of the Northern Rivers Regional Rugby League, 2019. *(Ursula Bentley/@CapturedAus)*

My tattoos, which cause plenty of comment. There are still a few blank spaces to fill!

7

GREEN AND GOLD

Mad Monday had a pleasant twist that year. Instead of getting blind drunk—which is the age old rugby league custom—I took it easy the day after the 2010 grand final, commiserating with the boys in our former teammate Daniel Conn's apartment at Coogee.

We were all licking our wounds from the previous night and I was chatting with my former Raiders teammate Jarrod Croker, who had come up to Sydney to support me in the big game. Suddenly my phone rang and someone from the NRL—I was in such a daze I can't even remember who it was—told me that I had been selected in the Australian team for the Four Nations tournament.

I couldn't believe it. At first I thought it was someone playing a practical joke on me but then after a few minutes, I realised it was fair dinkum. Again, my joy was tinged with sadness—I knew how much it would have meant to Dad to see me in the green and gold, running out onto the field. But for the rest of my family, especially Mum, I was delighted, and I think she shed a tear or two when I told her the news.

We had a 25-man squad under Tim 'Sheensy' Sheens and he told me straight up at the start that I was only going to get one game. We had some great halves in Cooper Cronk, Darren Lockyer and Kurt Gidley so I understood and accepted that—one game for Australia is a dream come true for me.

I assumed I'd be playing against Papua New Guinea, a game we would win fairly easily, and again, that was fine by me. So you can imagine my shock when in the lead-up to the big game against New Zealand at the famous Eden Park in Auckland, Sheensy said to me, 'This is it—are you ready?' I think I just grunted and nodded my head as I came to terms with what Tim had just told me. It was going to be a daunting task facing the strong Kiwi team on home soil.

Putting on the green and gold jersey in the sheds before the game and then singing 'Advance Australia Fair' ranks as number two of the finest moments of my life—things I will never forget if I live to the age of 100. Stuff I can hopefully one day tell my grandkids.

We met a pretty hot Kiwi side who were all fired up on home soil playing in front of a capacity crowd and they really took the game to us. Their team had a host of NRL experience and proven match-winners like Benji Marshall, Issac Luke and my Roosters teammates Shaun Kenny-Dowall and Sam Perrett. I was alongside Cooper Cronk in the halves and what an amazing player he is. He controlled the whole game from start to finish—with a little help from his Storm teammate Cameron Smith—and the two of them dictated terms. I didn't do a lot—I didn't have to do a lot because these two guys ran the show, and I just took a back seat.

We eventually wore them down to win 34–20. But a week later the two teams met again in the final in Brisbane and I lost my place, with the maestro Darren Lockyer coming back in at five-eighth alongside Cronk. The Aussies went in as huge favourites but, as they often do, the Kiwis lifted their game and really stunned the Kangaroos with their aggressive approach. It was anyone's game in the dying stages, with a try to Nathan Fien 60 seconds from full-time giving the Kiwis a thrilling 16–12 win.

Coming on top of the grand final loss, it ended a bitter-sweet season for me, but it was my best year in the game nonetheless and I thought I had really arrived as a top-class playmaker capable of winning games on the day.

At a dinner during the tournament, I was named International Player of the Year—a massive honour when you look at the blokes I beat for the award from England, New Zealand and our own ranks in Australia. I felt like my return to the game was now well and truly complete. That Aussie jersey is one of my most prized possessions. I've given away plenty of my shirts over the years, to mates or for charity events, but that is one I will never part with. Mum is looking after it for me at the moment but once my career is over and I've settled down somewhere, I'm going to have it framed and put it straight in the pool room, as they say. I've done plenty of good and plenty of bad in my life, but that is something no one can ever take away from me—having the honour of playing for my country, even if it was only the one game. It was a moment of immense pride for me and my family and those who have stuck solid to me and helped me along in my journey. That one game meant the world to a kid from Goulburn who'd had to jump plenty of hurdles along the way—many of which were self-inflicted—and more than once I thought I would never get to this level, or even close to it.

I was still pretty young and took a lot of it for granted during the tournament, being surrounded by so many great players and being at the highest level of the game. I didn't appreciate it as much as I should have but, older and wiser, I do now and can say with pride that I was a Kangaroo.

•

During that year the *Daily Telegraph* newspaper had a campaign to show the dangers of reckless driving in an attempt to bring down the road toll. They asked me to take part in it and so I went through my 'shame' file. By then I had my licence back and was driving more responsibly. I realised that the consequences of some of my actions behind the wheel could have been far worse than having a contract torn up or even going to jail. I could have killed myself—or some other innocent person on the road. I believe I am not a bad person at heart and have always accepted responsibility for my actions. The *Telegraph* ran a full page of me talking about my 'sins' on the road and hopefully the message got through to some young blokes who read it. It's embarrassing to see all the stuff you have done wrong, but if it saved even one life, it was well worth telling the painful tale.

Around that time I started dating television presenter Liz Cantor. We met on a breast cancer charity walk earlier that year and there was chemistry there. We kept in touch and started dating when the Four Nations were on. We got on well but it was a long distance relationship, as she was on the Gold Coast and I was in Sydney. It's hard to maintain relationships over that sort of distance, especially when you both have busy schedules, and it didn't last, but we parted as friends.

The year finished on a bit of a bizarre note. In the off-season I got back on the drink, as you do, and after one late night I couldn't find my apartment keys. I had a two-storey townhouse at Coogee, so in my intoxicated state I thought, 'This is easy, I'll just climb up onto the balcony and jump in the window.' Sadly my body was not in a good way after more than a few beers and as I was climbing up, I lost my balance and fell square on my back. It didn't hurt too much but I did get quite a nasty gash on my hip from the fall and had to go to hospital to get stitched up. As they prepared me, they pulled down my shorts—and found my keys in my undies! Yet another example of the evils of getting on the drink. It seemed I would never learn.

•

If 2010 was the high point of my career, 2011 was a nightmare of a year. It started badly when I got pulled over for a random breath test by the cops early one morning. I was actually on my way to sign a new deal with my finance manager and mate Trent Tavoletti, and Roosters boss Nick Politis. I'd had a few drinks the previous night and, as I was back on a probationary licence, I wasn't allowed to have any alcohol in my system. So the cops were cool, they understood I wasn't drunk but had some alcohol in me from the night before—but they still had to charge me. Of course the media found out and I was front page headlines again—and Roosters management wasn't impressed.

I got an extra break from training because I had played in the Four Nations and also had a groin operation, so my preparation for 2011 wasn't ideal. When I got back to the Roosters, Smithy called me and Mitchell Pearce into his office. He tore strips off us both—especially me. He reckoned I had let myself go too much over the off-season and had let both him and the club down. But what really hurt is that he said I didn't deserve the Dally M the year before and only got it as a 'feel good' story for the game and the media, it was a vote of sympathy after all I had been through.

I was stunned. I wasn't in bad shape, I just let my hair down a little over my break, as most players do. His words cut deep. He was the first bloke to congratulate me for winning the Dally M and now this. I didn't know what to say but felt like getting the bookshelf in his office and tipping it on his head. I was furious and thought his nasty words were totally unwarranted.

Shattered, I went home and called my manager Dave Riolo and he rang Politis and told him about the meeting. A few hours later, Smithy came around to my apartment and rang the doorbell. I didn't want to let him in—I wanted nothing to do with him. But I buzzed him up and he did apologise. I felt like he only did so because he was ordered to by Politis, who I always got on well with. The bad blood with Brian Smith remained there in some form for the rest of our time together at the club. That's pretty much how Brian Smith was, a prickly character who could be your best mate one minute and at your throat the next.

I wasn't happy at the Roosters from that point, and in April 2011 I lost my shit and went on a bender with my new teammate Anthony Watts. We finished up at Kings Cross at a bad hour and of course the media were all over it.

Anthony had allegedly assaulted his then girlfriend so they tore up his contract on the spot. I thought I was headed for the same fate but I came clean with chief executive Steve Noyce. I told him I was in a bad head space and that I hit the booze out of frustration to try to forget my problems for a few hours.

I was on a grog ban and fully expected to get the boot, but Nick Politis has treated me well and loves a good redemption story. A few years earlier, he would have been well within his rights to give Jake Friend the heave-ho after several indiscretions on the drink. But the club believed in Jake, helped him turn his life around and he became a club captain and a tremendous role model. Maybe Nick thought they could do the same for me, I don't know.

I got read the riot act—yet again—and stood down for a few weeks to get a mental health assessment and take stock of my career. Steve Noyce even told me not to attend the big Roosters–Dragons ANZAC Day clash the following week and that really hurt—not being there to support my mates. It made me feel like a leper.

NRL boss David Gallop decided to put his two cents worth in. 'With Todd Carney, things are complicated,' Gallop told the world in a press conference. 'It is his reckless disregard for undertakings [about not drinking alcohol] that is perhaps the most alarming aspect of where he is at. That to me is very disturbing and shows he needs some serious help.' Gallop called me in to League HQ for a talking to and I really couldn't say too much in my defence. I'd broken the rules and the Roosters arranged for me to go to Alcoholics Anonymous.

I went to a few meetings but didn't feel comfortable there. Despite my problems on the drink, I wasn't an alcoholic—I didn't get up every day and start drinking at 10 a.m.

My problem was more the binge drinking, and the things I would get up to when I got full of beer. It was interesting hearing the other blokes' stories, but I decided it wasn't for me. Also, I found out that stuff I was saying there was getting back to the club—a major breach of the rules of Alcoholics Anonymous and a point of major concern for me. I was pouring my heart out to a bunch of guys and somehow it was getting back to my employers.

I got some support from an unlikely source around the same time—Kings Cross identity John Ibrahim. John was a big Roosters fan and a bloke who was capable of making his own headlines for bad boy stuff on occasion. He went in to bat for me on social media and the press of course saw it and made a story out of it. But he begged the club to go easy on me and I appreciate it—thanks, John.

Desperate to get me back on track, the club sent me off for counselling, and I gave that a go. But the bloke wanted to put me on medication and I didn't like the sound of that. So the counselling didn't last for long. I had problems, sure, but medicating me so I would become a zombie, walking around without being my normal self, was not the answer in my eyes. Plus there is no telling how it would have affected my performance on the football field or at training. You need your wits about you out there and no way was I going to go out there medicated and not myself.

I'm a big believer in the theory that if you want to get through something, you have to want to do it and ultimately do it yourself. You can have all the support in the world but at the end of the day, it's up to you to take the right steps. The club told me, 'Blame your bad behaviour on your dad's death and the media and public will go easy to you.' But I wasn't about to do that. Sure it was a factor in me going off the rails but at the end of the day, you are responsible for your own actions. Sometimes you just want to run away and hide, but you have to face the music and get on with your life and try to be a better person. I know I was a slow learner in my youth, but I think I'm a better person now and have finally learned from my mistakes and learned that actions have consequences.

I was finally reinstated by the Roosters after a few weeks of soul-searching. I was glad to be playing footy again, but our season continued to go downhill and we struggled after losing the grand final the year before. We had a lot of injuries in the forwards and that really hit us for six. The man who really did the hard yards, Jared Waerea-Hargreaves, managed just eleven games. My great mate and future New South Wales captain Boyd Cordner only played six. Mitchy Aubusson, the heart and soul of the club, only got in six as well. Another of the big blokes, Marty Kennedy, did little better with eight. We had to blood a bunch of young forwards and they took time to get up to the pace of the NRL, which is to be expected.

I had plenty of pressure on me being the reigning Dally M medallist and was heavily marked every time I ran around the paddock. I also had a few niggling injuries which kept me out and I was probably lucky to get sixteen games in.

My fallout with Brian Smith didn't help. We patched things up to some extent as the season went on but I could never quite forgive or forget how he attacked me for no good reason. It had become a toxic relationship—on both sides. And when you don't get on with a coach, it's hard to run through brick walls for him.

I had troubles off the field too. I appeared in court on the latest drink-driving charge and managed to keep my licence but with strict conditions. That was in April, and the following weekend I had a shocker against the Warriors as they outmuscled us 24–12. In the press conference, Smithy said the off-field stuff was having an effect on my game— and he was probably right. It's hard to concentrate when you have bad stuff hanging over your head and a horde of cameras waiting for you outside courtrooms.

We won just ten out of 24 games that season and finished a very disappointing 11th on the ladder. After going all the way to the big one the previous year, it was agony watching the entire final series without even lacing on a boot.

You can find help from some of the most unexpected people at times when you are down. Michael Clarke was always one of my favourite cricketers and we met up once by chance at the Sydney Football Stadium cafe. He's a big league fan; growing up in Sydney's west he always supported the Magpies and then the Wests Tigers. But he immediately took an interest in me and took on a bit of a mentoring role with me in my time of need. I was somewhat in awe of him—the Australian Test cricket captain, the second most important man in the country behind the prime minister, as it has often been said, watching over me and caring about my problems. He said he really liked the way I played the game and I'll never forget a compliment like that from a bloke I respected so much. He knew more than most about the responsibilities a high-profile sportsman faced. If only I had listened to him more!

Late in the 2011 season, me, Nate Myles and Frank-Paul Nuuausala went on a road trip up north. The club had the squad on a two-week drinking ban and by the time we got back from Newcastle we had built up a bit of a thirst. We went to a pub in Darlinghurst for a couple of quiet ales. There was no drama, no atrocities, no complaints, but, as is the way these days, someone took a photo of us and it exploded on social media.

That was the final straw for the Roosters and they decided to cut me loose. To Nick Politis's credit, he didn't sack me, we agreed to make it a mutual release and that made it easier to get a contract at the Sharks. He had a chat to me and said pretty much that this was the end of the road and it was probably best for both parties that I left. He said to me, 'Just get a club and I'll release you.'

So when the Sharks showed some interest to my manager Dave Riolo, the Roosters just let me go without any complications. People still say I was sacked, and will always believe that, but it wasn't the case. In reality we had just parted ways due to a long list of off-field incidents starting with Brian Smith's spray.

I felt sad leaving the Roosters. I enjoyed the club, I liked living in the area and I played some of my best footy there. But again, I was my worst enemy and let myself down. Living in Sydney's east, there were a lot of temptations and, as you can probably gather, it doesn't take much to tempt me!

Of course the newspapers had a field day with the whole saga. The *Daily Telegraph* ran a massive 'From hero to zero' headline—just what you want to wake up to when your career feels like it is going down the toilet. The paper quoted Steve Noyce, who was to give me further grief down the track, as saying, 'It's disappointing . . . Todd is a decent human being but at the end of the day, we have to make a decision about the whole of the club. The club is bigger than one individual. It's a difficult decision but it's one that needed to be made.' Ironically, a year later, the Roosters sacked Noyce after another poor season, and Smithy for good measure. As I've said before, rugby league can be a cruel game.

I was again in limbo for a while. English and French clubs wanted me, but again I had trouble getting a visa because of my record. The Dragons showed interest and my manager Dave teed up a meeting with the great Wayne Bennett. I was more nervous than if I was meeting the Queen. The bloke has such an aura and I'd never met him before— I wasn't sure if he was going to tear strips off me because he has such a reputation for being a strict disciplinarian. But as we shook hands, he could sense I was nervous and just told me a joke and cracked a smile to ease my anxiety.

We had a good chat but they had Jamie Soward—who'd played a key role in the Dragons beating us in the 2010 grand final—and I didn't fancy playing second fiddle to him. He was well established in the team and I couldn't see Wayne dropping him for me. The talks didn't come to anything, but I could see why players hold Wayne in such high esteem. He was genuinely interested in me and what made me tick and it was an honour to spend some time with him.

That left Cronulla as my best hope, and I have to thank Paul Gallen for the role he played in getting me there.

'Gal' was a bit of a wild child when he was a young player and for a while he was public enemy number one with the media and some fans with his 'take no prisoners' attitude, on and off the field. But he really turned his life around to become an inspirational captain at Cronulla and for New South Wales and is a great role model for the game. Gal really stuck his neck out to get me to the Sharks—even though we barely knew each other—and I can't thank him enough for that. I guess he identified with me for the strife I got into and he believed in second and third chances, because he had been down and out himself and knew players can change.

Gal pushed me onto club management and in October Dave Riolo and I signed a two-year deal at the Sharks on fairly decent money. My football life was back on track—and I was determined not to screw up this time. I used my time off wisely, joining my mate Roger Fabri's sprint academy and really working on my speed and acceleration. I ran with his elite crew and while they were many yards quicker than me, they took me in and nursed me along. That off-season, just before I joined Cronulla, I felt I was at the fittest stage of my career.

MITCHELL PEARCE

Carney had played some of the best football of his career alongside another wild child, Mitchell Pearce, in 2010, as the pair guided the Roosters from the wooden spoon to the grand final, where they were ultimately outclassed by Wayne Bennett's St George Illawarra. A larrikin in the Carney mould who also often found himself embroiled in scandal with the media and his club, Pearce formed an instant connection with Todd.

Even though they haven't played alongside each other at club level for nearly a decade, the pair remain firm friends. 'Toddy is around three years older than me but right through my schoolboy days I was aware of him,' Pearce recalls. 'Everyone was talking about this cool kid from Canberra with the tattoos and an amazing ability to play what was in front of him. We never got to play against each other because of the age difference but eventually got to come face to face when I made first grade with the Roosters around 2007. He was an established first-grader by then and every time we played the Raiders, I knew I had to bring my A-game because this guy was something special. He had the rare combination of speed and the ability to steer a team around the park and I was kind of in awe of him. When the Roosters told me we had signed him for 2010, I was over the moon. I knew him a little on a personal level by then, but more than anything I was excited at teaming up with him on the field. He started his career with us that year at fullback and he made me look good. He'd chime into the back line and with his blinding speed and ability to get through a gap, he'd steam onto my passes and create havoc. Mid-season, our coach Brian Smith moved him into the halves and it was then that we really got to do some great stuff together. After the disappointments of the previous year, we were winning games and much of that was due to Toddy's brilliance and we all fed off it. He won the Dally M Medal that year and deservedly so. We formed a special bond on and off the field and I count him among my closest friends.'

Pearce believes the pair shared almost a psychic connection. 'We were going to a party one night and decided to meet up at my place and go together,' Pearce recalls. '[Todd] walked in the door and I couldn't believe it. He was wearing the same colour shirt as me, the same colour pants and the same shoes. We laughed our heads off. I was going to change, but didn't—it was too funny. When we got to the party, no one believed that it was sheer accident that we were dressed identically. They all thought we were pulling some kind of prank. And it was the same on the field. This special chemistry just developed between us. For example, I would all of a sudden decide to switch the attack to the left or right and he would be there—it was just uncanny. When he left the club, I was shattered because we had formed such a close bond and he brought out the best in me and the team.'

Pearce admits that Carney is a complex individual. 'He has always lived life on the edge and never done things by half,' Pearce says. 'But at the same time he was just a bit of a joker, not a dickhead, and he is a loyal guy who is actually quite shy—nothing like he is portrayed in the media. He is a colourful character and always fun to be around.'

8

SHARK ATTACK

The pressure was intense from the moment I got to the Sharks. It seemed everyone—especially the media and the smart-arses—wanted me to screw up once again. But I found an immediate ally in Paul Gallen. 'Gal' is a club legend and a much-loved player in the shire, and a bloke who has had to fight his own demons. He put a lot of faith in me and tried to take some of the pressure off me.

'When Todd is at his best, playing good footy and is happy, there is no other player in the game that can do what he can on the field,' Gallen said in the pre-season. 'For a bloke who gets so much attention no matter what he does, he copes quite well with it all and doesn't get too flustered. I think the club has done pretty well. They've let him be who he is. He's an adult now. He knows that any wrong decisions he makes could affect the rest of his life because he's probably on his last chance. He probably doesn't need everyone to be talking to him about that every day. He's a smart bloke and a good bloke and he's doing well for us in training. Hopefully he lets his footy do the talking.'

It was a warm welcome from the skipper, but once again I regret not paying more attention and taking the words to heart . . .

•

Good things were happening that year, and it was around then that I met Lauryn Eagle. Like me, she was a bit of a wild child who found her share of strife, and she was also an elite athlete—a fine boxer and champion water skier— so we had sport and fitness in common as well.

I'd like to say it was love at first sight, but she didn't want a bar of me when we met at a Lonsdale sportswear launch. We were both brand ambassadors for the company. But we kept bumping into each other and eventually I won her over. I think it was in Melbourne during State of Origin there that we really established a strong bond, and I was touched that she was in the crowd cheering for me.

She happened to be there at the same time preparing for a fight and we spent our down time together.

Lauryn wasn't a rugby league fan and I wasn't a boxing fan, but we went to each other's events to give one another moral support. I did start to show an interest in boxing after seeing her go through all her stuff and that is what led to my charity match a few years later. We eventually moved in together in an apartment at Gymea near Cronulla and enjoyed some good times. I was ringside when she beat the previously undefeated Kiangsak Sithsaithong with a fifth-round TKO to win the World Boxing Foundation women's super featherweight title and I was so excited for her. I knew how hard she had worked to get there and it was a dream come true for her. Boxing is a tough sport and women have had to battle hard to get the recognition they deserve and she did a lot to establish the sport in Australia with her performances and the publicity they attracted.

We tried to deny anything was going on between us at first because we knew the tabloid press would have a field day with the relationship. Of course, in this modern era there are no secrets and it was fodder for all the gossip columns when the news eventually came out that we were an item. But after several months we found that two professional athletes who both travel a lot and have to train hard on different schedules don't make for perfect partners.

People move on and change interests and that is what happened to us. The massive media spotlight on the pair of us and the pressure that created didn't help things either. After a few months we parted amicably, though we stay in touch and still talk on occasion.

•

As I look back on my career, despite all the dramas, I think a change of clubs every two or three years was good for me, and is for most players in general. You can't help but admire one club players like Darren Lockyer and Andrew Johns, but I found a new environment, new players, coaches and ideas every few years freshened me up and gave me new spark.

After a disappointing second season with the Roosters, my first year with the Sharks in 2012 was a good one. They partnered me with Wade Graham in the halves and we clicked pretty quickly. Wade is a great mate and a very underrated footballer. While our body shapes and styles are very different, we both had similar games in that we liked to play what was in front of us and chance our arm if the opportunity presented itself. Shane 'Flanno' Flanagan would let us try something if we thought a chance was 'on'. He was less into structure than some other coaches I have had and I really appreciated that, and so did 'Wado'.

I got off on the right foot in my first hit-out in Cronulla colours in the trials—we smashed a pretty good Manly team 38–6 and I bagged two tries. That was the perfect way to get my confidence back after the stress of leaving the Roosters and having to start anew. I scored again on debut against the Tigers in Round 1, but we were pipped at the post 17–16. Then Newcastle scored an upset 18–6 win over us in Round 2 and we were suddenly staring at the worst possible start to the season, on the bottom of the ladder after the second round.

Coach Flanagan and skipper Paul Gallen called for some soul-searching and we had a huge game against Manly in Round 3. The boys rallied and we got up in another tight one 17–14, and that was a real turning point in our season: 0–3 would have been disastrous.

We were suddenly a team with confidence and reeled off six straight wins before a very good Souths team gave us a lesson, beating us 34–28 in Round 9. But by that stage we were well entrenched in the top eight and despite some hiccups along the way, kept our place there.

Unfortunately, it was one of those years where we appeared to peak too soon—we lost seven of our last nine games and tumbled out of the finals in the first week, going down to Canberra 34–16 and knowing we were well below our best.

To make matters worse, I snapped my Achilles tendon midway through the game and finished the day in hospital. Some days are diamonds, others are rocks—this was definitely the latter.

Overall, I had some good and bad moments during 2012 and was happy with my first season at Shark Park. I led the team in try assists and felt it was a good start, with the dramas of Smithy and the Roosters behind me.

PAUL GALLEN

Cronulla legend Paul Gallen supported Todd Carney before the pair had even met. No stranger to controversy himself during his long career, Gallen used his high profile in the media to beg for leniency for the troubled star during his dark days at Canberra.

'I'd only played against Todd a couple of times back in his early days in Canberra when he was just this rising kid,' Gallen recalls. 'I didn't know much about him—other than that he had a huge amount of potential and talent. When he got into trouble down there and the Raiders kicked him out, and then the NRL wouldn't let him join a rival club, I thought that was a shame. He had clearly done the wrong thing but he was young and young people can do silly things, especially if they drink too much or fall in with the wrong crowd. So I just tried to get across that you shouldn't throw a young player out of the game but should try to mentor and educate him. Of course I had no idea at the time that one day years later Todd and I would be teammates at Cronulla and when Todd got there, I think he was grateful that I lent him some support at a time when so many people were calling for his head.'

When the pair became teammates at the Sharks in 2012, they developed an instant rapport. 'Toddy is one of the game's great characters at a time when there are less and less characters in our sport,' Gallen says. 'I think he played some of his best football at Cronulla because he made a lot of mates there in a short space of time and felt very comfortable at the club— we are a low-key bunch with no big heads or airs and graces and he fitted in well.

'[Todd] enjoys life and, yes, more than once he has gone overboard and caused drama but he doesn't mean any harm and just goes a little crazy on the drink. He could handle his drink up to a certain point but after that, he was hopeless. And he never seemed to know when that point was, although I think he is better now. He gets crucified in the press and by the keyboard warriors on social media but sadly that's the world we live in these days. There are a lot of people just waiting for someone with a profile and a history of scandal to screw up and unfortunately Todd fits the bill. Those who don't know him probably think he is a dickhead but he is extremely popular with his teammates and generous with his friends. When it comes to his turn to shout at the pub, he'll come back with 45 drinks, he wants everyone to be happy.

'I've been around football for a long time and seen a lot of players come and go but I don't think I've ever seen anyone attract the attention that Todd does. It's like he is a little puppy—mischievous but loveable and everyone wants to talk to him and have their photo taken with him. He is always in the spotlight but he handles it very well. He does a lot of good out there, but because he does it out of the generosity of his heart and not for the cameras, most people never know about it.'

Gallen's one fear for his former teammate is that in years to come, Carney might be haunted by 'what might have been'. 'The guy had a very good career, but ultimately it was cut short by the silly things he did and that has to hurt,' Gallen says. 'He could do it all—his running game, kicking game and passing game were all top class. He played the one Test for Australia and three State of Origins but if he'd been a "cleanskin", he could have played so many more of both. I have played with few players with more natural talent—and the speed to go on with it once he carved open the defence. Unfortunately for him, he played in an era of political correctness and at a time when the game got tough on repeat offenders. Some people had it in for him and he bore the brunt of this blitz on so-called "bad boys". I just hope he doesn't get to the age of 40 or 50 and look back on his career and say, "Geez, I never quite fulfilled my potential." But I know him pretty well and he is a positive person. He has always owned up to his mistakes and has plans for the future so I think he'll be right. Todd is the type of guy who has been knocked down plenty of times, but has a knack of landing back on his feet. He is no dummy, either—he owns a bunch of properties and has mapped out a future in business for himself—again the real Todd Carney is very different to the one the fans think they know by reading the bad stuff about him in the press and on social media.'

9

BLUE BOY

The other big event in my career in 2012 was my State of Origin call-up for New South Wales—another of the proudest moments of my life. I remember watching those epic Origin battles in the early 1990s on the lounge in my pyjamas with Dad, telling him, 'One day I will play for the Blues.' As a kid you have dreams like that, and I see now that I was probably one of hundreds of thousands of young fellas with the same dream who told their dads the same thing. The difference is that I was lucky enough to actually make it—and what a thrill it was.

Ricky Stuart called me up and told me I was in. He was one of my idols when I was a kid so getting the news straight from him made it that that much sweeter. I think I have 'Gal' to thank a lot for me getting the nod over some other in-form halves at the time. Gal saw what I could do firsthand at Cronulla and helped convince Ricky that I was the right man for the job. Game one was in Melbourne and Ricky and his selectors picked a pretty new-look Blues team after years of Queensland domination. James Tamou, Tony Williams, Jamie Buhrer and I all came in for our debuts. Four new boys is a lot in Origin football, where experience is everything and you can easily get overwhelmed by all the hype if you are not used to it. Queensland, by contrast, stuck with the blokes who kept doing the job for them year after year and had just one new boy—Matt Gillett—a good player who had plenty of experience under his belt for the Broncos.

Ricky was great to play under. When I came in he promised me I would not be a 'one game Origin wonder', a fate which had fallen upon plenty of New South Wales players in the past. I had to admit, the thought had gone through my head. I was worried if I had a 'shocker', it would be my first and last State of Origin jersey and I'd never play Origin football again. He promised me, come hell or high water, that he would stick with me for the series, so not to stress out about getting the arse after game one. Later on, I found out he did the identical thing with Jamie Soward the previous year, and he and Mitchell Pearce were the Blues halves throughout the series. That was the first time the Blues had kept the same halves for nine years, whereas Queensland seemed to keep basically the same combination year after year. Ricky had substituted me for Soward and kept 'Pearcey', my old Roosters teammate.

Mitch and I had a lot in common. We'd both had some hard times to get through and had our critics, on and off the field. We helped the Roosters go from wooden spooners to grand finalists in my first year at the Roosters and became best buddies along the way. Earlier in 2012, Mitch played for City and I played for Country in the annual fixture and we both went okay. This played a big part in us being selected for the ultimate test against the all-conquering Maroons.

I was a bundle of nerves before that first game, which is unusual for me, I'm normally pretty relaxed before a match. But I find, in hindsight, that most of my highlights are a blur. You live in the moment and things happen so fast you can't appreciate them at the time. Part of it is probably the adrenaline kicking in. As the call 'fifteen minutes for kickers' came, I looked down and I was still in my suit pants. I was on another planet, my mind a whirl of emotions and nerves. I rushed to get ready and having Pearcey next to me eased my anxiety somewhat. We'd played the last couple of seasons together and had some good combinations, and knew each other's strengths and weaknesses well.

Sadly, my muddled preparation in the rooms before the game pretty much summed up my night. They say that in your first Origin you are like a deer in the headlights. It is so much quicker and more intense than week-to-week NRL football, that you will struggle to keep up—and that was how I found it. The big crowd, the bright lights, the hype and the great Queensland team we were playing all combined to make it too much for me. I remember the first hit I took—it wasn't high but I felt I had been concussed, it was that hard. The self-doubt grew. The voice inside my head said, 'You don't deserve to be here,' and I couldn't shut it out.

Queensland had Cooper Cronk and Johnathan Thurston—two of the all-time greats—in the halves and that only made it more daunting. I was something of a passenger and just let the game get away from me. I had very little impact.

Despite my problems, the game itself was pretty close. Akuila Uate scored an early try for us from a bomb and I had the chance to make it 6–0, but the kick was from way out near the sideline and I scuffed it. Again, in a normal club game, I might have landed it, but the pressure was just so full-on.

As with most Origins, the game was a powderkeg just waiting for the first bloke to toss a match at it. It all erupted midway through the first half and the forwards from both sides got stuck into each other. This was in the days of the 'punch and you go to the sin bin' rule, so it was mainly just pushing, shoving and swearing. I stayed out of it—I have always been a lover and not a fighter—but our centre Mick Jennings couldn't resist. He ran twenty metres to punch his opposite number Brent Tate in the head and when order was restored, he got sent to the sin bin for ten minutes to cool his heels.

It was a rush of blood but it cost us dearly. The Queenslanders, with so much class and experience, made full use of their extra man, with Darius Boyd scoring in the corner. Thurston landed one of his booming conversions and we were suddenly down 6–4. As they so often do, Queensland scored again just before the break—again through Boyd. We found ourselves shell-shocked at 12–4 as we walked back into the sheds after more than matching them for most of the half.

Ricky fired us up at half-time and emphasised how we had to score next—and we went out determined to do just that. Soon after the resumption, another bomb brought us dividends, with Jennings scoring to put us right back in the hunt at 12–10 after I landed the conversion. We could have drawn level soon afterwards when I had a long-range shot at a penalty goal, but it sailed just wide of the posts.

It stayed that way until ten minutes to go, a real old-fashioned wrestling match, with both teams capable of taking it. But with just seven minutes left, they scored a highly controversial try. Greg Inglis juggled a kick ahead and it bounced off our hooker Robbie Farah's boot and back to Greg. We thought it was a knock on, no question. The video ref had a zillion looks at it before declaring that Farah had played at the ball intentionally, thereby not making it a knock on. Our captain Paul Gallen was livid and argued with the on-field referees but it had little to do with them. The blokes in the video box, Ben Cummins and Matt Cecchin, made the decision and the refs just shrugged their shoulders. Ricky was fuming after the game too—that decision killed off any chance of us coming back, and for the fourth series in a row, Queensland led 1–0 and held the whip hand.

Ricky kept good his promise and I retained my spot for the second game despite my less-than-spectacular debut. It meant a lot to me for two reasons. Firstly, it showed that the selectors had faith in me and secondly, the game was in Sydney, my home state, and I knew I would have heaps of friends and family at the ground—as well as 80,000 screaming supporters in a sea of blue.

We had a real fire in our bellies after the circumstances of the loss in game one and ripped into them from the outset. I felt more comfortable—I'd got that tough first game out of my system and the cheers of the crowd at ANZ Stadium made us all feel ten feet tall. I was getting plenty of support from people I respected, too, like Andrew Johns, probably the best halfback of the modern era. We didn't really know each other well but he sent me a few texts after game one, knowing the anxiety I was going through and the self-doubts after my below-par performance, and that helped a lot. 'You could tell by his body language that Todd was nervous in game one,' he told the press—and he was spot-on. 'Now he's got that game out of his system, he will be better for it. I'm expecting him to really come into his own in Sydney.'

Brad Fittler, another boyhood hero and Blues legend, was also great with messages of encouragement. Come game time, it was a tense start, scoreless for the first twenty minutes or so but then the game opened up. Our fullback Brett Stewart found some space and dived over in the corner for the opening try. We were on top—as we had been for periods of the first half of game one—but went to half-time behind again. After holding them out for almost the entire half, we failed to clean up a bomb just before the hooter. Their prop Ben Hannant picked up the scraps and before we knew it, it was 6–4 Queensland.

Early in the second half we were on the attack and I saw their fullback Billy Slater was slightly out of position. I put in a grubber kick and was all set to regather it and score near the posts—I could already smell the six points. But just as I was about to dive on the ball, the old fox Cronk took my legs out from under me. It could have been a penalty try, but they are few and far between, especially in Origin football. The refs did send Cronk to the bin, however, and from the subsequent penalty, I kicked the goal and we levelled at 6–all.

Things started to go our way. The maroons lost Slater and Corey Parker to injury and were feeling the heat a man down. I could sense this was our chance to put the knife in. I saw a gap in their defence and went for it, getting through their line and finding Brett Stewart in support, as he raced over for his second try.

Then, while they were still down to twelve men, Jarryd Hayne made a big bust and Josh Morris sprinted away for the try. We were 16–6 ahead and although Queensland had come back from similar situations many times in the past, we were pumped and determined they were not going to do it to us again, especially in front of our home fans. They did peg one try back when Inglis dived over, and came close again when Tate looked set to score. But Jennings, the villain in game one, became the hero this time when he knocked the ball out of Tate's hands.

We hung on for 16–12 and that full-time siren was one of the sweetest sounds of my life. The crowd went berserk and we lapped it up—the hairs on the back of my neck still tingle when I think about it—we had beaten an absolute champion team and done it in style, holding them out in the dying stages and preventing one of those traditional Queensland comebacks that they love to boast about north of the border. I sometimes watch the video of that game when I am a little down and it brings a smile to my face. One pressure conversion in particular that I landed from wide out really pumps me up—it was among the best kicks of my life.

The celebrations in the room were pretty wild after the win but Ricky was quick to remind us that though we had squared the series we still had one hurdle: taking on the Maroons in the decider on their home patch—the dreaded Suncorp Stadium—in front of 50,000 parochial Queenslanders.

Meanwhile, the premiership went on. Ricky had said something to me a few weeks earlier which stuck with me—that the really good Origin players back up after Origin and still produce the goods at club level. So, four nights after that great win, I found myself lining up for the Sharks at a cold, wet and windy Shark Park in front of fewer than 10,000 fans, in a weakened team against a near full-strength Warriors side. We were missing Gal, who couldn't back up from Origin with his dicky knee, as well as Wade Graham and Andrew Fifita, who had been rushed in for emergency appendix surgery. Without our three best forwards, we were really up against it.

The Warriors sensed we were vulnerable and dominated much of the match, leading 17–6 at one point in the second half. But I was able to put on a couple of big plays, my mate in the halves, Jeff Robson, scored two tries and we snuck home 20–19 for a vital and courageous win.

'Robbo' and I had formed a very effective combination even though we were a completely different style of half, with our strengths and weaknesses. He was an old pro who could really read a game and control the team. That gave me greater freedom to play my own individual game and not have to worry about structures and the like. While my best year was probably my Dally M year at the Roosters in 2010, I believe I played my most consistent football at the Sharks over the course of my time there.

I was in a good place when we headed north to Suncorp Stadium for the State of Origin decider. I'd played there a few times before but Origin was an entirely new beast, as I quickly came to realise when we flew into Brisbane. From the moment we landed, we were seen as 'the enemy' and copped glares and abusive comments everywhere we went. And the boos from the mob as we ran onto the stadium were enough to send chills down your spine— to say it was intimidating does not even begin to describe the atmosphere. But Ricky had played plenty of Origins up there and he warned us what to expect, and told us that the hate would only make us stronger as a group and create a tighter bond.

We had a siege mentality and things started well. I landed an early penalty goal and then Brett Morris scored one of his trademark tries on the wing, and with my conversion we were flying at 8–0. But then the brilliant Thurston sprung into action. He threw a superb cut-out pass to Darius Boyd—who seemed to score every time he put on a Queensland jumper—and he went over in the corner. Then Thurston made a break from deep in his own territory and our defence was shot to bits. Two tackles later, 'JT' got the ball back off Corey Parker and scored an easy try next to the posts, and suddenly our nice lead had evaporated.

Soon afterwards Justin Hodges crossed for the Maroons, but he ran behind a couple of his own players and we screamed to the referees for obstruction. They sent it upstairs and we were confident that the video ref would disallow the try. But after looking at it a heap of times, he flashed the green light. We were dumbfounded. All season long, similar incidents resulted in a penalty to the defending team—now, in the biggest game of the year, it was a try. Gal again vented his frustration at the refs on the field, and it was the same story—they said 'it's not our call' and put it on the blokes in the box. It was 16–8 at the break and we headed into the rooms knowing we had a massive mountain to climb if we were to take the series.

Brett Stewart was a try-scoring freak at club level for Manly and he got us back into the game early in the second half. He pounced on a grubber from our hooker Robbie Farah, with my conversion reducing the deficit to 16–14. But Thurston landed two penalty goals to extend their lead to 20–14 with ten minutes to go. Things weren't looking good but then Farah put up a cross kick and Josh Morris jumped above Darius Boyd to grab the ball and ground it before being barrelled over the sideline. That left me with a pressure conversion to level the scores from the touchline and the crowd were giving it to me as I lined up the vital attempt. I went through my processes and tried to block them out, telling myself, 'You can do this' . . . and nailed it.

We thought we had the momentum going into the last few minutes but with six minutes left, the Maroons got in good field position and Cronk landed a field goal. Our hearts sank, but there was still time to snatch a win or take it to extra time. Pearcey had a long-range snap at field goal in the final minute but it went agonisingly wide, then the hooter broke our hearts. Queensland had done it again, though by the narrowest of margins, and it was a bitter pill to swallow. It was their seventh straight series win and I have no doubt in years to come, their team will be remembered as being among the all-time greats of Origin football.

I take a lot of pride out of the fact that we pushed them all the way and came within a point of squaring the series, but in the end their big match experience and ability to come up with the pressure plays made the difference.

•

Late that season some prick who had it in for me started a rumour that I had failed a drug test. It was just another grub with no life of his own trying to stick the knife into me and I simply dismissed the rumours. Even when it was all over social media, I ignored it. My coach Shane Flanagan and my teammates, my family and the NRL knew there was nothing to it. But I was furious when this bloke somehow got Mum's number and started calling her. I had to draw the line.

I came out swinging in the media, declaring it was all bullshit and daring this gutless bloke to come forward with some proof—because I knew he didn't have any. I reassured Mum there was nothing to it and I hated the stress it caused her. I'm a big boy and can take any shit people throw at me. I've been doing it all through my career and I acknowledge I've brought a lot of the rubbish that I cop on myself, but when you involve my family, that's a whole different story. No way do my family deserve this grief and I hate these grubs for inflicting it on them.

I also had a meeting with my sponsors around the same time and they asked me about the rumours—the whispers had spread right through the rugby league world. Whoever was trying to ruin my life was doing a bloody good job of it. Again, I had to defend myself and set the record straight, it was causing me more grief I didn't need. People don't realise or care how damaging shit like that can be, especially to a bloke like me with so many strikes against my name.

Social media is fun at times and a good way to interact with the fans, but it can also be vicious and unforgiving. I can see why a lot of players have nothing to do with it, which is a shame for the fans. If the wrong person had believed those rumours about me, it could have been the end of my career then and there. 'Flanno' was great, coming out and declaring the rumours to be complete garbage. The ridiculous thing was this was mid-season and I hadn't been drug tested since February that year, when I'd been given the all clear.

I asked people for advice and they said just ignore it and it will go away. But the rumours had spread like wildfire, so I slammed the talk and gave it to the bloke—whoever he was—in the media. He needs to get a life. The rumours are dead and buried, but sadly some people will always believe what they want to and the mud stuck for quite a while, until the low-life found someone else to crucify.

It seemed people couldn't get enough of the highs and lows of Todd Carney. I got asked to appear on a Channel 10 sports show later in 2012 to talk about my problems with the drink and I thought it might do some good for young blokes in a similar situation to know my story. They just asked me about my career and the issues I had with alcohol and I answered as honestly as I could and thought nothing more of it. I've never considered my life to be that interesting or remarkable. I'm just a footy player who slipped up a few times too many for his own good and got smashed for it. But the feedback was amazing—the show got its highest-ever ratings of 176,000 viewers and the producers were delighted. The usual pricks had a crack at me over it, but overall I got a very positive reaction and it made me realise that, down the track, if I improved my confidence and manner of speaking in front of the cameras, maybe I could help young people to avoid the mistakes I had made.

JEFF ROBSON

Jeff Robson and Todd Carney could be described as chalk and cheese—on and off the field. Out in the middle, Robson was a veteran tradesman, often going unnoticed by the critics as he steered the Sharks team around the park in a quiet, professional manner. Alongside him, Carney was the explosive force who would wait for his chance and carve up the opposition defence. And off the field, Robson was a cleanskin, playing fourteen seasons and nearly 200 games in the NRL without so much as a hint of trouble. The fact that the two talk about each other like brothers shows, again, that there is a very different side to Carney than the public is led to believe.

'I really liked my time at Cronulla with Todd, he was a character and life was never dull with him around,' Robson says. 'We used to hang out a lot in our down time. The difference between us was that I was married at the time and "the boss" would tell me when to come home. Todd was younger and wilder than me and he would always stay out just that little bit too long and that occasionally landed him in trouble.

'We always had great banter and are mates for life. We don't see a lot of each other these days but talk on the phone regularly. I consider him like a brother, even though we are such different personalities. I really feel for him because he is one of the most genuine and nice guys I met in football, until he lost his way when he had too much to drink. Then he lost control and it cost him a lot in terms of his football career.'

Robson remembers one memorable day at Sharks training when Carney amused his teammates with his antics. 'We went out for dinner the night before and had a few drinks—maybe a few too many,' Robson says. 'Then Todd couldn't sleep so he took a few sleeping tablets. We didn't start until noon the next day but when he arrived, we could tell he wasn't right. His eyes were rolling, he was speaking in gibberish and dropping weights. We asked if he was okay and he insisted he was all good, so from there we went to King Wan, the famous Chinese restaurant at the Leagues Club and again, he wasn't himself. He was very boisterous, which is unusual for Todd, he is normally pretty sedate and quiet.

'Things got worse when we had a video session after that. We were preparing to play Canberra and Todd got to his feet and started yelling "We have to watch this player and that player cutting into the backline." It was hilarious because the players he was referring to weren't even in the team we were about to face! Then Todd wanted to get out onto the field but our coach Shane Flanagan wanted to address the boys. Todd had had enough sitting around and yelled, "Geez, can he hurry up?" I don't think Flanno saw the funny side, but we were pissing ourselves. Finally we got out onto the field and did ladder running drills. Todd still wasn't himself and his arms and legs were going all over the place—he got jumbled up in the ladder and ended up in a mess on the ground. We started a catch-pass drill . . . and he dropped every ball. At that stage, our trainer Trent Elkin pulled Todd aside and said, "I think it's time you went home, mate," and sent the poor guy on his way, getting someone to drive him home.'

Robson played some of his best football in his time at the Sharks alongside Carney. 'We had a great understanding and our differing styles worked well together for the team,' Robson, now a welfare officer for the Wests Tigers, says. 'I would just do my thing and move the team upfield and then he would cut loose—and when he cut loose, he was dynamic. I played alongside a lot of halfbacks in my career and Todd was as good as they come. He had it all—speed, strength, a great kicking game and the ability to read the play. He won us plenty of games virtually on his own and there are very few players in the NRL good enough to do that. He had all the talent in the world and when he was on his game, there were few better.'

Like many of his Cronulla teammates, Robson was shattered when the Sharks sacked Carney after the now infamous 'bubbler' photo went viral in 2014. 'We played the Broncos that week and Todd had an absolute blinder—he was scoring tries, setting up tries and kicking goals from all over the park,' Robson says. 'It was as good a game as he played in his career. What disappointed us as players was that we found out he was sacked via the media. I was watching FOX Sports when it came up as a news flash. We weren't even consulted or warned what was going to happen and when you look at what players do today, the punishment was way out of proportion to the crime. They could have fined him or suspended him but to just boot him out of the game, basically for life, was ridiculous. And they have never forgiven him or given him the opportunity to come back into the NRL, which is a real shame—even after he did three or four years in Super League. The thing I respect about Todd, he just copped it on the chin and has got on with his life.'

Robson is certain that his former halves partner will make a successful coach. 'People who don't know Todd just think of him as a boofheaded footballer because of what they read in the media,' Robson says. 'He actually has a great football brain and an aura about him where young blokes gravitate to him. They know he has been in trouble but they respect him for what he has done—winning the Dally M and playing for Australia. He has gained a lot of wisdom over the years and one thing for sure, he can tell young blokes what *not* to do if they want to make it to the top.'

10

ACHING ACHILLES

The Achilles injury made my 2012–13 off-season a very disrupted one. But I have always been a quick healer and my ex-girlfriend Lauryn helped me through it. Having an elite athlete to train with made things easier and I was very grateful to her for nursing me through a tough period. I spent a lot of time in the hyperbaric chamber and also did altitude training, which was hard work but sped up the recovery process.

I was back on the field for Round 1 in 2013, which was my goal over the summer, so I was pretty pleased. I hadn't lost much speed but took a few weeks to get my fitness and confidence back, which is only natural after such a major and painful injury. I owe a debt of thanks to renowned sprint trainer Roger Fabri. Roger and I worked together at the Roosters and he is the best in the business. I knew I would need some professional assistance and Roger was only too glad to help out. After my NRL days were over, Roger gave me a job in his junior academy, coaching young kids in speed and the fundamentals of the game, and he opened my eyes to a whole new world. I'm keen to get involved in a similar style role in the bush, as I feel so many country kids could benefit from a person who has had NRL experience and it would be my way to put something back into the game that has given me so much. I actually plan to model it for kids playing all sports—anything that requires speed and agility. Rugby league is obviously my bread and butter though and I'll be tailoring special training routines for fullbacks, halves and hookers—the key decision-makers on the field.

Getting back to 2013, we played the Titans in the first game and squeezed out a 12–10 win which we made harder for ourselves than it need have been. But winning first up is always a massive boost and my Achilles came through fine, much to my relief. The first hurdle was over. We followed that victory with a close defeat to the Rabbitohs and a win over the Warriors. Round 4 was the big local derby against the Dragons and we came crashing back down to earth, losing 25–12.

I was still the current New South Wales five-eighth and, as such, was starting to get interest from rival clubs early in 2013. Both the Dragons and the Panthers put good deals on the table, while the Warriors also wanted me and the money was certainly tempting. I met with the Warriors—who were coached by my old mate Matty Elliott—while I was in Auckland to watch Lauryn and Paul Gallen in a charity boxing match. Matty came up with a very attractive offer, as well as the opportunity to play outside Shaun Johnson, as James Maloney had just left the club. But I thought I owed Cronulla—they had taken a gamble on me and I wasn't about to walk out on them after just a couple of seasons. I was also playing well in a strong team and my view has always been 'If it ain't broke, don't fix it'. I could have got more money elsewhere but I have never really been a 'money person' and believe in just trying to live your life and be happy.

I had all but agreed to re-sign with Sharks football manager Darren Mooney but things hit a speed bump. He was sacked for his role in the peptides scandal and talks ground to a halt. I was left in limbo, having knocked back the other offers I'd received I was set to put pen to paper at the Sharks when all bets were suddenly off. Cronulla were like a rudderless ship with Mooney gone and the future of several other officials was under a cloud. After several weeks of not knowing where things were at, the new management of the club signed me up for four more years at Shark Park. In the end, obviously unbeknown to me or anyone else at the time, I would only play out a fraction of that contract.

•

My form was fairly solid once my confidence came back from my injury layoff and I was keen to regain my Origin spot and help the boys end Queensland's long dominance at the elite level. I thought I would have been better in my second series after learning a lot the previous year, but I suffered a knee injury around selection time and it never happened. And while the Achilles problems were gone, I began to have hamstring troubles and they were very frustrating. For a bloke who relies on his pace, these injuries were a killer, and also affected my confidence. Every time I hit full speed, that little voice in my head said 'Be careful, your hamstrings may tear.' The mind is such a powerful force in sport—often it can make or break you in the big games.

James Maloney got my New South Wales number six jumper and I couldn't argue. He was playing out of his skin for the Roosters and later in the year helped them to win the grand final. He's a class act and a renowned big game player.

I kept my focus on the Sharks and we had another strong season, finishing fifth on the ladder with fourteen wins and ten losses from our 24 games. Michael Gordon was our number-one goal-kicker and he did a great job—I was more than happy to hand the pressure job to him. But Mick got hurt late in the season so I was given the role again. After having had a bit of a break from kicking I was back in the saddle and, for some reason that I can't explain, was hitting them as well as at any stage of my career. Goal-kicking is all about confidence, and after landing a couple of booming conversions from near the sideline there was no stopping me. At one stage I had the stats of 28 goals from 29 attempts and a couple of them helped us win close games in the lead-up to the finals.

We were pitted against a strong Cowboys team in week one of the finals, and in a controversial game edged them out 20–18. But there were plenty of complaints from up north after the game when it was discovered that our winger Beau Ryan had scored a vital try on the seventh tackle. I felt for the Cowboys—it was a cruel way to get knocked out of the finals but that's footy. Some weeks luck smiles on you and others you feel like a black cat walked in front of you.

I tore my hamstring late in the game and, try as hard as I did all week, I couldn't get it right for the following weekend against Manly. I even went to see a specialist, Dr Chris Mortensen, who believed he could get the hamstring right using a revolutionary electronic device that he attached to the muscle. World surfing champion Layne Beachley had used it to good effect when she suffered a similar injury and I was so desperate I was prepared to try anything. But the leg still didn't feel right on game day and I reluctantly pulled out, hoping the team could win without me and I'd be right the following week.

The boys put up a brave showing against the Sea Eagles, but went down 24–18. Once again the Sharks were right up there all year, but the hope of that elusive first premiership was dashed. My season was pretty strong—I was named Dally M five-eighth of the year for the second time and led the team in try assists and line-break assists. But I have to put my hand up and admit that I also had the most errors at Cronulla that season, so perhaps I was guilty of pushing things a little too hard and attempting things when it would have been better to hang on to the ball. But I always believed in playing what was in front of me and trying something if a try was 'on', and my coaches supported me in that most of the time. So while I could look good if the miracle pass or kick came off, I'd feel like a goose if it didn't—such is the role of the modern play-maker in the NRL.

•

There were dramas aplenty for the Sharks in 2014 when the peptides scandal exploded onto the front pages of newspapers around the country. It all began in 2011 when players began being treated by a guy called Dr Stephen Dank, a sports scientist.

In 2013, the Australian Sports Anti-Doping Authority and World Anti-Doping Agency began a lengthy investigation into the club and the practices of Dr Dank and whether players and officials realised that he was giving the players peptides, substances which were banned throughout the sporting world, to boost injury recovery and improve performance.

Fortunately for me, all of this happened before I got to the club and I wasn't involved in the whole sorry saga. But I felt for the boys as they went through hell and when I attended meetings with them, I felt their pain. It was clear to me that they were confused about the whole thing and felt they had been let down by people who they had trusted—both inside the club and on Dank's side.

The doping authorities had the boys in their crosshairs—they wanted a high-profile scalp and a bunch of rugby league players fitted the bill perfectly. I know only too well what it is like to have the cameras following your every move and having your name dragged through the mud by both the media and the fan in the street. It can be very damaging to your self-esteem and psychological wellbeing. There have been times in my career when I just didn't want to leave the house and my Cronulla teammates were now in that horrible position.

I honestly believe that the players weren't told the full story at the time. The club officials told them to go see Dr Dank and as professional athletes we tend to do what we are told and not ask as many questions as we should. Also, we are footballers, not doctors or chemists—try reading the label of some of those supplements and you would be flat out pronouncing the names of the ingredients, let alone knowing what they are and whether they are on a banned list or not. Your coach and officials have the power to cut you and even end your career at any time, so you do what you are told and try not to rock the boat.

Dank told the boys that he could make them better players and help them overcome injury quicker, and the club gave it all the green light. The boys did not believe their own club would make them do anything that was illegal. If they had their time again, I'm sure they wouldn't have gone along with it but, at the time, they did what their employer told them to do without question, as most people in most industries would do.

I did have one brief brush with Dr Dank though, after I snapped my Achilles tendon in 2012. The club sent me to his clinic to determine if he could speed up my recovery. I went to see him at Bondi Junction but I had a bad feeling the moment I walked into the waiting room. There were a lot of plastic surgery patients there—fake boobs, lips and the like.

I saw the doc and he took some blood tests, saying he believed he could fast-track my return to the field from the injury. He told me a bunch of techno babble and I nodded in agreement like an idiot—it was like he was speaking a foreign language. He was wearing a nice white coat and I was in a doctor's surgery . . . who was I to argue? He asked if I was good with it all and I nodded in agreement, as by then my head was aching from all the fancy words he had used.

I had an appointment to go back the following week and get down to the business of being treated. A few days before the second appointment, the boys were out having a drink and I told Paul Gallen about my experience. This was, of course, before the whole thing exploded so, like the rest of the boys, I had no idea how wrong it all was and how the poop was about to hit the fan. Gal gave me a strange look, pulled me in close to him and whispered into my ear, 'Don't go back to him [Dank], whatever you do.' He didn't explain why—he didn't need to—the look on his face was enough to freak me out and I cancelled the appointment the very next day and I had nothing else to do with the man.

So that is one occasion when having a beer actually *saved* me from strife—and probably the only time. In the end, fourteen players were suspended and several staff given the sack for their roles in the whole thing. Most of the boys accepted back-dated twelve-month bans, which in effect meant they only missed a few games at the end of the season, while Flanno was outed for twelve months. I'm convinced that with my record and the way officials had it in for me, I would have been given 108 years if I'd had any involvement in the affair!

I managed to get my driver's licence back midway through that year, but even that wasn't without drama. It was written into my contract that I got a car once my suspension was up, but Toyota, who were sponsoring the club, didn't want to give me some wheels because of my poor driving record. Enter Madeline Tynan, a powerful businesswoman and big supporter of the Sharks. She learned of my dilemma and was good enough to let me use a Jeep four-wheel drive. Madeline owned a big dealership in the shire and I was very grateful to her. I made sure when I eventually gave back the car it was in pristine condition.

On the field, it was a disastrous year for the club with all this going on. The boys naturally found it difficult to focus and keep their minds on the job, both at training and in matches. They had bigger things to worry about—possible five-year bans that in a lot of cases would have all but ended their careers and stained their reputations as 'drug cheats' for all time. We won just five of our 24 games and finished a long last on the ladder with the wooden spoon. The place was at an all-time low all year, with morale at rock bottom. But while I had dodged a bullet that time, my world was to come crashing down midway through the following season.

11

THE BUBBLER

I've had plenty of highs and lows in my life, but things really took a dive one weekend in June of 2014. The writing was starting to go on the wall a couple of months earlier when Steve Noyce, who was now the Sharks CEO, called me in and fined me $5000 for turning up at training slightly hungover from a big night. But that was only the beginning. The funny thing with this was he never notified my managers David Riolo or Trent Tavoletti of the breach; he said later that he gave me a copy of the breach, which I have no memory of.

On 27 June we played the Broncos in Brisbane on a Friday night and it was an epic match. We were mid-table and it was a vital game for us. It was up at Suncorp where they are always hard to beat and we started poorly with the big crowd cheering them on and their attacking machine in full power. But the tide began to turn at half-time and, after being behind by nearly twenty points, we stormed home to win 24–22. I scored a try and set one up, so was well satisfied with my efforts; those are always the best games, when you are going badly and staring defeat in the face but manage to turn it around into a win. It is a sign of character and grit and all players cherish those moments. We came back to Sydney and I went to bed all happy with my efforts, unaware my life was about to be turned upside down overnight.

A week earlier, my flatmate Nathan Gardner and I had gone out to Northies, the well-known watering hole in Cronulla, and had a few beers. That was it, or so I thought. But the night after the Broncos game I got a text with a photo of myself from Trent with the words 'what the hell?' I looked at the phone and was horrified—I saw a picture of myself doing 'the bubbler', an optical illusion where it looks like you are drinking your own urine, in the men's room at Northies. I had no recollection of performing the act yet there it was in living colour before my eyes.

I asked myself, 'Where is this . . . is that really me . . . when did I do this?' There have been plenty of mornings when I have woken up thinking, 'How did I get home? What did I get up to last night?' That was one of my big problems on the drink—I basically blanked out. It's not a good feeling and often I would look at my phone the next morning for clues as to what I had been up to. Invariably there had been text messages and photos which gave me some indication of what I had done. But it was never anything like this.

I thought at the time it was just some random pic and it would all go away. But it didn't. The next morning I woke up to my phone exploding. People were texting and calling me telling me the photo had gone viral and the media were having a field day with it. I was horrified. I didn't remember doing 'the bubbler', much less having it photographed—and how it got on social media all around the world remains a mystery to me.

Slowly the memories started to return and I remembered being a little drunk at Northies and going to the bathroom with this bloke, Mick Robinson, who was just a random— I wouldn't even call him a mate—a blow-in who liked to hang out with the players. Without my knowledge, Robinson took a photo of me doing 'the bubbler' with his phone, which I did not see nor did he tell me he had taken it. The shock that this photo ended up on social media was even more disappointing. Robinson has tried to talk to me and apologise a few times, but I have just brushed him off. He reckons he sent the photo to his brother and then his brother lost his phone and someone found it and sold the photo to the media. It sounded like a pack of lies and I still don't believe a word of it. He admitted in an interview that he took the photo without my knowledge and said he never meant to cause me any harm, but clearly he did the wrong thing by me, and while there is no excuse for my actions, had he not filmed what happened in a private place, my career would never have been in ruins.

It was a stupid party trick, very tasteless and inappropriate, but I feel it needs to be put in context. It was at no one else's expense and I was just acting the fool. And my rights were violated—if anyone else had a photo of them taken in a toilet and circulated around the world, they would get some sympathy, not be criticised. The main thing I felt was shame. I knew I would have to call my mum and explain it all to her and my sisters and they would cop the fallout from it all once it became front page news. At the time everything was a whirlwind, so I asked Trent if he could call Mum and the girls until I could contact them later. I was sure they had seen the photos already, and, sure enough, my younger sister Melinda had.

Early the next morning 'Flanno', who was suspended for a year and supposed to have no contact with the Sharks, sent

Dave Riolo a message saying, 'We have a problem.' Flanno was one of the few people who stood by me, and a few months later, again while he was suspended, he met with me and Dave and devised a plan to get me back to the club the next year. The chairman Damian Keogh was also on board with getting me back, but sadly it came to nought—I can only assume they were overruled by the board. The club wasted no time getting the wheels in motion to sack me. Noyce spoke to Nathan Gardner, questioning him about what had happened. Once the call was over, Nathan warned me, 'He's coming to see you,' in an ominous voice. This was the next morning and, sure enough, Noyce called on the phone and said he had better come around and talk to me about it all. Noyce was CEO of the Roosters when they sacked me, so we had some pretty ordinary history to start with. But right on 11.30 a.m. he arrived at the door acting like my best mate and we talked.

He asked me to explain it and, really, I had no answers. I was ashamed and embarrassed for myself, my family, the club and the game. I had this feeling that they were going to sack me and asked Noyce straight out if they were going to tear up my contract. He could see I was distressed and in a bad way and he reassured me. He said not to worry, that the club would handle it. I begged him not to sack me—I knew if they did it would effectively end my career in Australia, if not everywhere. He promised me that everything would be okay, that it would just blow over and, silly me, I believed him.

'The bubbler' was nothing new at Cronulla—one of the boys performed it regularly after a win for a few laughs. Noyce left me alone after we talked it through and, feeling relieved, I didn't think too much more about it for a few hours.

Trent Tavoletti had organised a meeting with Noyce, as Dave Riolo was away interstate. Trent arrived at the club around 2 p.m., and the first question he asked Noyce was, 'Has he been sacked? The media are reporting left, right and centre that he has been.' Noyce advised Trent that no decision had been made and that he would tell Dave and Trent before any decision was announced, which gave me some form of relief. Trent asked Noyce to consider other forms of punishment besides the drastic step of cutting me; he said that would be throwing me to the wolves and it could have a dire effect on my mental wellbeing. Noyce assured him they were looking at all possibilities and that any decision would be made by the entire board.

Hearing all this, I was a mental wreck . . . I guess I tried to block it out. Later that day, while sitting at home with Nathan Gardner and Wade Graham, who was over to support me, Trent arrived to advise me what he had put to Noyce—basically a three-point plan rather than sacking me. The three points were:

1. Stand me down from playing for the rest of the year.
2. Fine me $250,000 to $300,000 (which would effectively mean I wouldn't be paid for the rest of the year).
3. Make me undergo community work within the shire to help re-instill the values of the club, myself and the game.

It became a waiting game, and we sat by the phone in anticipation of some form of response from the club. Around 5.10 p.m. Trent called Noyce to see where things were at, as the media reports kept stating that I had been sacked. Trent was concerned because before he walked in to see Noyce, veteran *Telegraph* journalist Phil Rothfield, who is close to the Sharks, walked out of the club—tell me this wasn't a coincidence.

Anyhow, Trent wanted to go home to his family, having been with us all day. Noyce advised Trent to hold off leaving, but that no decision had yet been made, as he was waiting to speak to Keogh and all of the board members. Noyce again assured Trent that no decision would be made until he had spoken to him or Dave, and not until the next morning at the earliest, as there were board members overseas. Trent didn't receive a call back from Noyce.

It was my phone that rang at 5.30 p.m. I answered on loudspeaker and Gardner, Graham and Trent could hear the entire phone call from Noyce.

My first question was 'Have I been sacked?'

Noyce advised that 'no decision' had been made, but asked me what I thought my punishment should be.

I told Noyce I would do anything, just please don't sack me because it would end my NRL career. I asked him if I could have the chance to sit in front of the board and discuss the situation with them and also talk to players and coaching staff.

Noyce told me to get some rest, and said we would talk tomorrow about a suitable punishment.

Positive news, so I thought.

Dave Riolo warned Noyce because of the 'history' he and I had at the Roosters, insofar as he was instrumental in my departure from the club, that there could be a perception of bias against him if he took action to sack me. Noyce assured Dave it was not the case but, again, I didn't believe it. Dave also rang Keogh, who said words to the effect of 'Initially I didn't think it was such a big deal, but after talking to Steve [Noyce] I've changed my mind.' But at the same time, Keogh assured Dave no decision had been made or would be made until a full board meeting was convened.

Just after my call with Noyce at 5.30 I had sent a text message to him asking what had happened. I wrote, 'Please don't rush into sacking me. That would be me finished.'

About 30 minutes after this Gardner's and Graham's phones received text messages. I asked the boys what was going on and they weren't sure exactly what it all meant. They had received an identical text from Rob Willis, the Sharks media manager, saying that the club board had made a decision and that no one was to make a comment on it to the media.

All of this was happening without me, Dave or Trent having any warning from Noyce . . . surely this couldn't be true? I rang Noyce at 6.30 and it was only then he told me that the club board had held a meeting and decided unanimously to sack me. I was stunned—this was the bloke who a few hours ago assured me that it was all alright and it would just blow over. I found out later that at 5.30, about an hour before, when I had asked Noyce what was happening, the club had posted a media release on its official website saying that I had been sacked.

Noyce told me that, apparently, the club had held an emergency board meeting, without even asking me or my manager to come along to explain what had happened— and decided to rip up my contract. We are talking more than four years left on my deal, worth about $3 million, but money was the last thing on my mind at that moment. And I didn't believe for a minute that the board decision was 'unanimous'. How was the board meeting unanimous when there were board members who couldn't be reached because they were overseas?

I spoke that same day to a guy called Craig Airey, who was on the board and a supporter of mine, and who was overseas at the time. He didn't even know I had been sacked. I explained the situation and fessed up to what I had done and he sent me this email: 'No I haven't [spoken to the board] I'm in London. I read an article this morning that said the board had decided to sack you. That's not true, it was decided by Keogh and Noyce. I was never asked for my opinion and neither were a number of others on the board. This decision will have repercussions for our "friend" [Noyce]. I am so sorry mate, I will do everything I possibly can, I'm back on the 19th July and be around to see you. If you need anything just contact me.' I trusted Craig and four days later he was in touch again via text:

> Ok mate, I'm in your corner I've run this past a few people I trust on the board and have their support, if you're catching your manager, the idea is to get you to apologise to NRL, Club and Fans and take responsibility,

(will need to get some wording), to enter some sort of counselling/Rehab (Sharks to Pay), to then have you involved in ordinary work, (my company, don't have to attended), then for Sharks to apply to NRL around Dec to have you reinstated around rounds 3 or 4 next year. Very rough outline at the moment and the less people know about it the better chance of success, I've had a long call with Keogh and he doesn't know I'm talking to you, but has agreed that if you can 'lay low, have no more f--k ups we may go back to NRL and see what happens', keep positive mate and hold your head high, if you were a nobody this wouldn't be a problem, don't let people look down at you, everyone's got something they regret, yours is just public.

It was clear he was trying to save my career, while others at the Sharks were trying to bury me. The same day he texted me again: 'Hi mate I've got the numbers on the board to support my reinstatement plan, just need to get it happening, I'm sure more than ever we can get you back for start of 2015!' That raised my hopes—but I still didn't trust elements on the board who I feel had it in for me.

I spoke to Gal, our captain, and he said to just cop it sweet and that they would probably go easy on me if I sat out the year and reinstate me the following season—but

I wasn't so confident. I was a wreck. I could see my career crumbling before my eyes, all because of my own idiocy, but also people at the club who wanted me out at any cost.

NRL boss Todd Greenberg weighed in and said I had brought the game into disrepute—he basically washed his hands of me. I get that I did the wrong thing, but it was just a stupid party prank. The NRL has gone a lot easier on players charged with rape and assault and other serious crimes, some who had even done jail time like Danny Wicks and Russell Packer. I was tried and convicted without even getting a chance to explain or apologise. Yes, I was an idiot, no argument, but it was a massive kick in the guts. I thought about legal appeals and the like but for the moment, I just had to cop it sweet. I took some time off and hoped it would all blow over as Craig had said it would.

Sadly, now, more than five years down the track, it hasn't. Like John Hopoate is always remembered for sticking his finger up the arse of rival players, Trevor Chappell has had to live with the underarm delivery for decades and Mike Tyson is renowned for biting an opponent's ear, 'the bubbler' is what people associate with Todd Carney. I'd clearly done something inappropriate but I was half cut at the time and no one was hurt by my actions—they were just dumb, plain and simple.

Sadly the public and media aren't so forgiving. Every time I go to a public toilet, I find myself anxious that blokes will see me in there and take the mickey out of me. It happened recently at the races. I was there minding my own business and there was a big queue to the men's room. Some young blokes full of ink spotted me and yelled, 'Carney give us a bubbler!' It was embarrassing and I just tried to ignore them. Next thing I knew three of the lads—none of whom I'd ever met—had whipped out their old fellas and were doing the bubbler right there in the open. People never cease to amaze me—these guys were bagging the shit out of me for something I did years ago and have publicly regretted and apologised for, and then they are doing it themselves! Yet because they weren't Todd Carney, they just zipped up their flies and got on with their day. I felt like saying, 'Guys, let it go—haven't you got anything better to do? How do you even remember that crap? It was years ago.'

When I did 'the bubbler', it changed my life forever and ended my career in the NRL, something I had worked so hard to achieve for many years. People still give it to me now about the incident—on the street and on social media. It is hard to take sometimes and gets me down. In fact, when we are at the pub and I need to have a leak, I'll try getting two or three of the boys to come with me, just for security.

My advisers were equally stunned that the club could sack me without even calling me in to front the board and state my case. A couple of days later we lodged an appeal to the NRL with a formal letter. The standard NRL contract states in black and white that if a club believes a player has gone against its standards, it must follow procedures, including the issuing of a breach notice, which the Sharks did not, and also that the player should have the right to appear before the board within five days. None of this happened. They just basically tossed me out onto the street. They never even gave me a letter of termination—I found out most of their actions through the media, which isn't right when you are talking about a bloke's livelihood. We argued that tearing up my contract was an 'unreasonable' punishment, that the club could have taken less drastic measures but failed to even consider them, as far as we could tell. Within less than 24 hours of the photo becoming public, they had punted me in what we deemed a knee-jerk reaction to public and media pressure. The chance to put my case and discuss alternate punishments never appeared to enter their minds—they just wanted to be rid of me as quickly as possible to take the pressure off them.

We would win the appeal with the NRL Appeals Committee in March 2015, where it was found that the Sharks hadn't followed due process according to the

NRL Players Agreement. It was now back before the Sharks board.

I finally got my hearing in front of them in April, nearly a year after I left the club. It was done via Skype as I was in France playing for Catalans and the club just went through the process of explaining why it had sacked me and gave me a chance to have my say. But there was little I could say or do—I'd moved on, signed with Catalans and was playing in Super League. The whole thing was a sham just put on by the club to cover its arse for its previous mistakes in not giving me a hearing. Two weeks later, they sent me a letter to officially confirm my sacking. It was a mixture of legal mumbo jumbo and platitudes in the hope that that would be the end of the matter. But for me, it wasn't that simple—the club denied me natural justice and threw me out on the street.

We had already won our appeal with the NRL Appeals Committee. That opened the way to take legal action against the Sharks because they did not observe due process before my dismissal. We proceeded to lodge an Unfair Dismissal claim with the NSW Supreme Court against the Sharks. A week before the case was to be heard—three years after the event—the Sharks and I agreed to an undisclosed settlement amount which cannot be talked about, as there were certain privacy rules put in place. *Case closed.*

It was a lengthy battle and the club clearly didn't take it seriously. They had not, in the opinion of my legal representatives, carried out due process when sacking me and the evidence in Craig's emails and texts clearly backed up my case. Apart from anything, the club contravened the Fair Work Act by not telling me I was sacked in writing—they didn't even do it by phone call or text. I had to ring Noyce myself to get the bad news. I'd also told Noyce that I wanted to front the Sharks board to apologise for the damage I'd done and work out a suitable punishment—that never happened.

The club claimed that I had breached the terms of the standard NRL contract that every player signs, namely:

i. engage in no conduct whatsoever that damages or may have the tendency to damage his reputation; and

ii. at all times during the term of the playing contract maintain a reputation for high standards of personal conduct, including a reputation for respect of women and children, the responsible consumption of any alcohol that he drinks and for lawful and good behaviour generally.

The club's legal eagles also stated:

Whilst under the influence of alcohol, posing and exhibiting himself to other persons in a urinal and urinating upwards and in a manner which suggested that he was urinating into his own mouth, is a disgusting and depraved act. The performance of that act in the presence of other persons was detrimental to the best interests of rugby league . . . [and that] impression has a tendency to turn away men, women and children and sponsors who may otherwise have supported rugby league.

There is no doubt it was an immature act, but as for performing it in front of 'other persons', there was only one other bloke in the bathroom—the guy who took the photo.

At the time, I had the dubious distinction of being the second most googled person in Australia in 2014 behind Schapelle Corby (see later on about my meeting with Schapelle). League is far from a national game and I am anything but a national star, so it goes to show a lot about the country we live in. And I'm pretty sure they were googling about 'the bubbler' and not my exploits on the football field.

I love Australia and I am a proud Australian, but people just can't seem to get enough scandal in this great country of ours. Maybe their own lives are boring and they find people like Schapelle and me, who end up in trouble, to be a source of fascination—I don't know. But hopefully people will google me less in the future!

How ridiculous that this is how my NRL career would end. While it's all in the past, I am also still bitter at the circumstances of the whole thing and the lies that were told. At the end of the day, I can blame no one but myself—I did something very stupid and paid a hefty penalty. But people do stupid things every day and, in most cases, they are forgiven and forgotten—and they can get on with their lives without their reputations and careers in tatters.

MUM

A battling, down-to-earth Aussie mum, Leanne still remembers with dread the night 'the bubbler' went viral, when her life fell apart along with her son's.

'I got a text at three o'clock in the morning from a friend with the photo and I was mortified,' she says. 'He'd just played probably the best game of his life against the Broncos . . . and now *this*. I managed to get in touch with him next morning and told him, "Toddy, you are REALLY in trouble . . . this is serious." He didn't even know what I was talking about—he just blacks out when he has a big night on the drink.

'Cronulla moved quickly to get him out of the place. One minute their chief executive Steve Noyce told him that it would be resolved and would blow over—that same day Todd had to call him to find out he had been sacked. They said they convened a full board meeting to make the decision but I know at least one board member was out of the country, so you have to wonder. Football clubs tell lies—and often get caught out. But there was nothing we could do—they had made up their minds and again, there was no thought of duty of care for him—there was some negative publicity so they just shoved him out the door. He was clearly in need of counselling and guidance but they weren't interested.

'The day Todd signed with Cronulla, I called him and said, "You realise that this is your last chance?" He knew it . . . but I don't think anyone could ever have foreseen that it would end the way it did—over a photo in a bathroom. Again, the whole thing caused the family a lot of grief. But you know what, at the end of the day, people are entitled to their opinions and if they want to bag him, it's their right. It's the world we live in. People love taking cheap shots at those who are up on a pedestal—sadly it's the Aussie way.

'Around that time I got a call from the Ray Hadley [radio] show asking if I would go on and defend Todd. I didn't think it would do any good so I declined and the producer asked, "Just tell me one thing—is he bipolar?" It would have been an easy excuse to say that yes, he was, or that he was depressed— a lot of players in strife seem to do that these days and it's a "get out of jail free" card, it seems. I said, "No, he's none of those things." Todd has always taken responsibility for his actions. He puts his hand up and says "Yep, I did it" and faces the consequences.'

12

BALI BLUES

Devastated at what had happened, I was lost and confused. Those close to me were worried about my wellbeing without playing football—the thing I loved doing most—and one of those was an old mate, businessman Dave Martin. He owned a cafe in Coogee as well as another in Bali called Stacks, and invited me over there for the bar's tenth anniversary. 'You are in a shit place right now. Let's get you out of Sydney and over to Bali,' he told me.

The Indonesian holiday island has always been one of my favourite places, so I thought, 'Why not?' It was good to get away, even though my dilemma was never far from my mind. I also took time out to visit a bunch of Aussie guys in jail over there and take them some training gear. My troubles were nothing compared to theirs and if I could bring a little sunshine into their lives, I was glad to do it. I was going to burn all my Sharks gear when they sacked me. Instead I gave it to these guys and they acted like I had given them bars of gold. Dave told me they were all footy fans and would appreciate a visit from a high-profile player.

Among those I saw were two members of the Bali Nine, Andrew Chan and Myuran Sukumaran. They really enjoyed talking footy and I was happy to spend time with them. It was difficult to know what to talk about with them, knowing that pretty soon they would be facing the firing squad. I did ask them when they would be executed and they shrugged and said, 'You never know. One day they just come up and tap you on the shoulder . . . and off you go.' That just rocked me and again, put my petty problems into perspective. Sure, they were drug smugglers, but if they had been caught in Australia, they would have done a few years in a much better jail than the hell hole they were in, and then be set free to get on with their lives. But these guys' days were numbered, and they knew it. When I said goodbye to them, it was very hard—for both them and me—knowing we would never see each other again. As it was, both were shot on the prison island of Nusakambangan around a year later, in April 2015. They were both in their early thirties—my age now—and I'll never forget them. Their deaths hit me hard, even though I knew it was inevitable.

Another photo, this time taken at Stacks, caused me more grief while I was over there. Well-known Aussie and alleged drug smuggler Schapelle Corby, who was then on parole, and her sister Mercedes came into the bar one day and we started chatting. Of course, someone snapped a photo of us, it went on to social media and then the newspapers back home got hold of it and things went berserk. I got hammered again—just for talking to two ladies in a public place.

To be honest, I spoke more to Mercedes then her more famous sister and we just chatted about life. I did talk to Schapelle a bit and we commiserated with each other about the strife that you can find yourself in and how best to handle it. Schapelle actually had no idea who I was—she'd been in jail for much of my career—but she listened with a sympathetic ear as I told her of the mess I'd put myself in. I was in a bad place and glad for a caring person who also had her own problems. I didn't want to ask her about her time in jail and her guilt or innocence, but I did talk to her about visiting the Bali Nine guys in jail and that experience. I always take people as I find them and not on reputation. If someone is nice to me, I am nice to them back, irrespective of their reputation or what they may or may not have done. That's just the way my mum and dad brought us up—it's common decency.

But I nonetheless copped it from the do-gooders over the photo. For some reason the Australian media decided it was inappropriate for me to talk to Schapelle and have my photo taken with her. It just made me mad—I felt like I couldn't win. Even in Bali, my every move was under scrutiny and people seemed to love sticking the knife in when I was vulnerable and at my lowest.

There was one funny incident on that trip. I got blind drunk on a big night out and was walking out of the toilets when I crashed into this gorgeous girl and sent her flying. She landed flat on her back and I felt awful for her—it was a total accident. She'd had plenty to drink too but was okay after the initial shock. She dusted herself off and we started talking. She was from Brazil and on her first visit to Bali. We exchanged numbers and agreed to meet up at the same beach the following night with both of our groups of friends. I was quite taken with her—a genuine Brazilian beauty—and on the way to the get-together I bought a cheap ring from one of the many roadside stalls in Bali. After we'd all had a few drinks, I got down on one knee and proposed to her—just as a bit of a joke—and gave her the ring. But what I didn't know was that one of the boys had taken a photo of the moment and put it on social media with the words 'HITCHED IN BALI'.

I eventually crashed back at our villa but, of course, the photo went viral overnight. It was on the news, some TV crews rocked up at Mum's place in Goulburn and asked her for a comment. She knew I was a practical joker and just laughed it off. 'Do you think Todd would get married to a stranger in Bali without his mum there?' she told them, but that didn't stop the media frenzy. I was still comatose when Wade Graham burst into my room next morning and said, 'You fool—what have you done?' I'd lost my phone and couldn't see the 'damage' myself but all the boys were getting calls asking what the hell was going on. It was just a silly holiday prank but again, some people in the media treated me like I was a bloody criminal.

The story is still on the News Limited website. They haven't even bothered to take it down now years later even though it's clearly incorrect. Under the huge head-line 'Former NRL bad boy Todd Carney marries blonde Brazilian bombshell Lilian Tagliari' it ran photos of the two of us and a big story about our 'shock' wedding. It started out with the words: 'FORMER NRL player and bad boy Todd Carney has tied the knot with blonde Brazilian bomb-shell Lilian Tagliari in Bali. The 29-year-old announced the news via his Instagram account overnight, with a photograph of himself with the tattooed beauty. Showing off a new nose ring, Carney wrote: "Hitched in Bali." The marriage came as a surprise to fans as the couple kept their relationship under wraps.' Google it and see! All the smart-arses ripped into me on social media—sometimes people really need to lighten up and not believe everything they read.

MARK DENNIS

'I've always been a big Sharks fan and about seven years ago started running an SP betting operation in Bali's largest sports bar, YBar. Soon after starting, there was a Sharks game on the television from Sydney and this bleached blonde woman in her fifties started screaming "GO TODD" at the top of her voice every time Todd Carney touched the ball. At half-time I approached her and introduced myself—and to my amazement it turned out to be Todd's mum, Leanne, who was on holiday in Bali. We soon became good mates and when Todd came over to Bali a few months later in the off season, he came in to say hi. We hit it straight off and he ended up staying with me and we became good buddies. Todd loves Bali—I think because he is just another Aussie tourist and can escape the media fishbowl of Sydney that has caused him so much grief—and comes over regularly, always making sure to pay me a visit.

'On New Year's Eve, 2004, my eighteen-year-old nephew Jason took his own life, leaving behind his twin brother Daniel, his sister Melissa and his mother Fiona to try to pick up the pieces. Each and every birthday of the twin left behind is always the same as can be expected—emotionally draining and incredibly sad. In 2013 when Todd was playing for the Sharks, I gave him a call just after he had finished training and asked him to do me the favour of going to my sister's place to visit my nephew, whose birthday it was that day. Todd asked me what the address was and said he would head straight there and pop in for a few minutes. Now to anyone who loves rugby league, especially kids, to have someone of Todd's status—love him or hate him—turn up unannounced at your front door at dinner time is nothing short of priceless. Needless to say this brought the biggest smiles to my family's faces, who are also Sharks tragics.

'As if that wasn't enough, Todd took some Sharks training gear with him, including signed boots, and gave them to Daniel and even stayed for dinner with my sister and her family. My nephew has had a tough life but will never forget that random act of kindness from a supposed rugby league "bad boy". Forget what you hear and read—this is the real Todd Carney—a bloke who will go the extra mile to help someone out without any fuss or media fanfare, just to brighten up that person's day. I know countless other stories of lovely things the guy has done but because he does it out of the kindness of his heart and not for headlines, people never hear of them.'

•

One thing that gave me some heart when I got back to the furnace of Sydney was when I picked up a copy of *Rugby League Week*. The popular weekly newspaper—which sadly died a couple of years ago—ran its annual players poll. I did the poll a few times in my career and it was always the one chance to say what we as players *really* thought about the issues in the game—because it was totally anonymous.

As players, we have it drilled into us during our careers by our clubs to give the media nothing to make a story out of and to toe the company line, and not let them know our honest thoughts. Anyway, of the 100 players polled, an overwhelming number thought I had been hard done by at Cronulla and that I should be reinstated as soon as possible. At possibly the lowest point of my life, it was a lovely vote of confidence from my peers and I can't thank them enough. It meant a lot to me.

13

FRENCH FOLLIES

I was at a loss as to what to do. All doors in Australia were closed to me, so my manager and I looked to the Super League in Europe. I ended up signing with the Catalans club and I stayed two seasons there in the south of France—no visa problems this time around.

It was a little daunting for a bush boy at first, as I flew out of Sydney and landed in Barcelona, Spain, in late 2014. There I was met by a club official who didn't speak a word of English—which was still more than I knew in French—and he drove me the two-and-a-half hours to the club's home base in the town of Perpignan. It was basically silence all the way. We tried to communicate but it was a waste of time and, again, I asked myself, 'What the hell have I got myself into here?'

I always thought I would play in the Super League at some point, but, like most Aussie players, I planned it to be at the end of my career. Here I was, aged 29 and still, in my opinion, in the prime of my career. However, as with other unexpected forks in the road during my career, I just decided to make the most of it and enjoy my time there.

After I settled in I had a great time in France, playing with fun guys from the NRL like Justin Horo, Glenn Stewart and Dave Taylor. We had a pretty good side and enjoyed some success, and it was pleasing to help spread the rugby league message to the people of France. Soccer is obviously the number one football code there, as it is in all of Europe, with rugby union second and league a poor third.

We won games, were competitive at home and drew fair crowds. The thing I liked most about that stint in the south of France, though, was being able to travel all over the continent in our down time. But, as always, I managed to find drama, such as on one cold night in Berlin when I learned that Europe can be a dangerous place, particularly for unsuspecting Aussie tourists.

Justin, Dave and I were wandering around when a guy came up to us; he could obviously tell we were strangers in a strange land. He asked in broken English if we wanted to buy some cheap perfume for our wives, girlfriends or mums. He said he had heaps of stuff like Chanel No. 5 at a fraction of what you would pay for it in the fancy stores. Before we knew it, we were following him down a dark alley into a very shonky-looking building where he and his mates had enough perfume to stock the shelves at Kmart several times over. We got a little carried away and all filled our arms with the stuff and, when it came time to settle, I whipped out my credit card. The bloke in charge gave me a filthy look and said, 'CASH ONLY!' We didn't have enough money between us, so he told Dave and Justin to stay there while two of his buddies went with me to an ATM to withdraw some cash. I had a bad feeling that these blokes were going to take the money—they were both built like gorillas and I'm only a little guy—and beat the shit out of me and bolt. I took out the cash and as they closed in on me, I put my hand in the pocket of my big thick jacket and said, 'No closer, I have gun . . . BANG, BANG.' They looked at me, shrugged their shoulders and kept their distance and took me back to the boys. We settled accounts and got out of there as fast as we could, but I often wonder what would have happened if I hadn't come up with that play. I'm lucky I've watched plenty of gangster movies in my time!

On the field, I played 30-odd games for Catalans. The season for me got off to a bad start when, in only my second game, against Salford, big forward Lama Tasi (a lovely guy who I played with at the Roosters) broke my ribs with a big hit. Tackling wasn't high on the priority list that day— the game finished in a 40-all draw. I had a few weeks off, because I wasn't about to make the same mistake I made at the Roosters of playing on and being below par, but came back and went okay at the club and stayed for two seasons. There was a lot of travel back and forth to away games in England and quite a few of the boys had language difficulties with refs and officials in France, but it was a great experience and I'm glad for having done it.

There was plenty of stuff that happened in France, and the beauty of it was that because no one really knew who we Aussie players were, it never made the headlines. I guess they pegged us for a bunch of silly tourists and ignored us. Once after a late night at a promotional event for the club, I flipped my car driving home . . . I think I fell asleep at the wheel. Luckily no one was hurt and I just left the car where it was and walked back to my place. But I forgot the keys were still in the car so I tried to climb up and through an open window on the first floor. It was the middle of the night and next thing I knew, a bunch of cops turned up with these big guns—I reckon a neighbour must have spotted me and dialled 000 (or whatever the emergency number is in France). Luckily, I managed to dodge them and walked to Michael Monaghan's house, which was just around the corner, and crashed there for the night. But it was a sponsor's car and they naturally weren't very happy, and I had to answer a few questions from the French police, which wasn't easy with the language differences.

Another time we had a weekend off and decided to go to Spain for a couple of days. We met this bloke who had a truck and took us to the Spanish border. There were a bunch of border police there and once the driver saw them, he screeched the truck to a halt, jumped out and just started running. The cops saw that and headed for the truck, so we all bolted as well, even though we had nothing to hide—we just panicked I guess. They caught the driver, he wasn't in very good shape, and I still don't know to this day why he bolted or what they charged him with, if anything. Because we scattered in all directions, no one knew where anyone else was. I was lost and alone on the border of France and Spain—not a good feeling. It was a long way back to our home base at Perpignan and I had little money, but I hitched a ride with a truck driver part of the way. I still didn't speak a word of French and he could only grunt in English, but he got me back in the right direction towards home and I managed to wing it the rest of the way.

14

FIGHT NIGHT

I had a ball in my two years in France, but the language problems and constant travel eventually got to me. I came back to Sydney and banged on the NRL door again, only to have it slammed in my face by Todd Greenberg and company. I was going to retire there and then but thought, 'No, bugger it, I'm not going to let them get the better of me.' So I signed with Salford Red Devils in England for 2017. Their owner Marwan Koukash was a flamboyant millionaire businessman and racehorse owner who had been trying to sign me for several seasons, so I finally said 'yes' to him.

Before heading off to Salford, though, I was back home in Sydney for the Christmas period when one morning my phone kept ringing off the hook. That's never been a good sign in my life and I dreaded to pick it up and see what was going on. But I thought, 'I stayed home last night . . . I can't be in trouble for playing up on the drink.' So I took a look at it to see what was going on.

It turned out that I was getting calls from a bunch of mates, geeing me up about putting on the boxing gloves. Paul Gallen was set to duke it out with Junior Paulo in a heavyweight charity fight night at the Hordern Pavilion. For some reason, little former Parramatta halfback Chris Sandow had challenged me to a fight on the undercard. I barely knew the bloke but I guess he figured he could beat me. I really don't know why he picked me out of all the blokes in the football world. Maybe because I didn't have an NRL club and was at a loose end.

I wasn't too keen to be honest—I'd never been a fighter and saw from my time with Lauryn that it is bloody hard work. But my mates put the pressure on me. 'You can't say no to him, it will look like you are scared,' they all told me. In truth, I think they all wanted to see me get my head punched in, but with all the pressure from them, and of course the media, I said 'okay'.

Things happened quickly from there. My co-writer Tony Adams is mates with Matt Rose—the brother of former cult hero George Rose—and Tony and I were having a coffee in

Coogee, catching up. Matt lived in the area, was passing by and sat down to join us for a latte—and half an hour later it was a done deal. It was against my better judgement, but it was for a good cause. I got some money but a fair chunk of the proceeds went to charity and the preparation would be good for my fitness, I reasoned. My nominated charity was Spark of Life, an arm of the Dementia Foundation, which raises money to find a cure for the horrible disease that cost me my dad. Hopefully, down the track, other families wouldn't have to undergo all the pain we went through in trying to cope with Dad's sad decline.

Mum didn't like the idea of her little boy getting the crap beat out of him. When she heard about the fight— and not from me because I wasn't about to tell her—she rang me up and yelled, 'What the heck are you doing? Have you lost your mind?'

She might have been right. I thought it would be just a muck around bout in headgear and there would be no real chance of getting hurt. But when I was signed and committed I found out it was to be fought under professional rules, with heavy eight-ounce gloves—and no headgear! I even had to get blood tests from a doctor to make sure I was up to a hard fight and had to get a NSW boxing licence.

I was definitely getting edgy the more I realised that this was no 'charity' bout and Sandow, who could always talk a good game, was telling anyone who would listen that he planned to punch my lights out. So I called a mate, Matt Gambin, who had been our boxing trainer at the Sharks. He started working with me and immediately realised I was going to prove a challenge for him. I also had to lose six or seven kilos for the fight and that was probably the hardest part of it all. I weighed 93 kilos and needed to get down to 86—it wasn't easy.

I started sparring with former Sharks hooker and good mate James Segeyaro. He didn't have a club either and he was as bad as me with the gloves on. I'd floor him, then a few seconds later he'd floor me. Matt could see it wasn't helping my style or confidence so he got a few professional fighters in to spar with me—now *that* was scary. Most of them went easy on me. They realised I was just a washed up rugby league player and a couple of them were kind and helped me with my technique. But this one bloke came and he meant business. He gave me a hiding and even with some thick headgear on, my ears were ringing for days. After we went a couple of rounds, he took his gear and got ready to leave and I whispered to Matt, 'Don't get him back . . . PLEASE!'

On the morning of the fight, we had a big public weigh-in, in front of a crowd of media and supporters. Chris was there too and I wanted to chat and say hi, but he wanted nothing to do with me—clearly he was taking this whole thing a lot more seriously than I was. I stepped on the scales and was half a kilo over the regulation weight. A little voice inside my head said, 'Great . . . fight off.' But it turned out that morning weigh-in was just for show—the *real* weigh-in was later in the day, close to fight time. So I went with Boyd Cordner, who I was living with at the time in Coogee, to the gym and we rode and rode the exercise bikes—my mind went back to that never-ending bike ride home on the back roads as a kid, with Dad driving behind us in his ute. After that, Boyd and I sat in the sauna for a couple of hours and sweated and sweated.

I was drained by the time we did the real weigh-in, but I managed to lose the half kilo . . . just. So it was game on—and I was a nervous wreck. I had Billy Dib in my back-up team but as we walked out to the ring in front of the big crowd, he saw this other bloke he couldn't cop—and he and his mates were into them. My whole support team deserted me to join in the stink and I walked up to the ring alone, with chaos all around me.

Boxing is intimidating—there is nowhere to hide in the square ring and if you get in trouble, there are no team-mates to help you get out of it. It is very gladiatorial, just you against a bloke trying to knock your block off, which is exactly what Sandow was attempting with me. A rough, cheeky character from outback Queensland, Chris came out swinging and I quickly realised he was quite used to employing his fists to settle disputes. This was definitely not his first fight. I had a height and reach advantage, but he was clearly the more experienced fighter. I felt out of my depth—even my bottom lip was quivering. My last fight had been in the playground—except for one behind a pub in Goulburn that I didn't even want to think about, as it hadn't ended well. I was basically trying to get out of the way as he swung a flurry of punches in my direction.

I managed to stay on my feet throughout the three two-minute rounds—which was one of my main aims—whereas Chris hit the deck twice. He reckons he just lost his feet, but I'd like to think I hit him so quickly he never saw it coming. In the end, the judges declared the bout a draw and I've got no argument with that.

It's something I can tick off my bucket list. I've been challenged to bouts a couple of more times since, but I've decided that if I step into the ring again, it will be against a fair dinkum boxer who knows what he is doing. While he will probably kick my arse, it will probably be more orderly. I've looked back at the bout a few times on video and it resembled a street fight more than a boxing match—two little blokes swinging wildly at each other with haymakers and not even a hint of style or grace. It was hardly 'the sweet science' and looked a totally different sport to the one that made the great Muhammad Ali famous. But we put our bodies on the line and I think the crowd enjoyed our boots 'n' all approach. It was pretty funny, and a very different world to the one I was used to—it definitely took me out of my comfort zone.

•

With the boxing match out of the way, I left the Aussie summer and headed back to the cold European winter in England in 2017. My timing in joining Salford could probably have been better. They had two of their marquee signings in the halves—Robert Lui and my old Canberra teammate Michael Dobson—and I felt a bit out in the cold there. It didn't help that in my first game after signing, I spent the entire 80 minutes on the bench—not the best way to make a new boy feel welcome!

I played around seventeen games that season but was plagued by calf troubles throughout. The calf is a frustrating injury—once you get it, it is hard to shake and only a long rest can ensure you have beaten it. And just when you think it feels fine, it can 'go' on you again and that was the case in my season at Salford—the cold weather and soft grounds only made things worse for my legs. I was upset I couldn't play my best football for Marwan, a good bloke and genuine lover of the game who has helped raise league's profile in England. It was a frustrating season. I only signed for one year and the club announced on social media that they weren't keeping me—not the ideal way to part company.

Even though I have plenty of baggers, I use social media a fair bit myself and fired back, saying I would have loved to stay on but that my contract wasn't renewed because of cutbacks, which is what they told me. So I put this message out on Twitter to let the fans know why I was leaving: 'I respected the team [and] the coach i never wanted to leave but the club asked me to leave to save money'. And with that, I packed my bags and left England for what I believed at the time was almost certainly the last time as a professional footballer.

15

HOME AGAIN

I realised at this point that it was now or never if I was to have any chance of one last crack at the NRL. I really wanted to go out on my own terms and not be dictated to by officials and bans and the like. So late in 2017, I signed with the Northern Pride, the feeder team for the North Queensland Cowboys in the Queensland Cup. I had an offer of around $1 million to stay in England from Hull Kingston Rovers and the Pride offer was around one-tenth of that! But I am a firm believer that money isn't everything—you have to be happy in your life—and I'd been away from friends and family for three long years.

There were nibbles from NRL clubs—Manly were supposedly keen and Ricky Stuart, who knew what I could produce from my brief stint under him in State of Origin years earlier, also showed some interest at Canberra. I wouldn't have minded going back to the Raiders, but the board blocked it—they thought there was too much bad blood and the like so they canned it. I was upset. I thought I'd served my time for my 'crime' after three years in Europe and begged for a chance to finish my career in the NRL. I made an impassioned plea in the press: 'I'll trial for a contract—I'm ready to do whatever it takes,' I said. 'I've been playing in England and France for the past few years but want to finish [my career] at home. My body is good and all I'm after is an opportunity. On grand final day, all the retiring players will be presented to the crowd. That sort of thing burns in my stomach—that is the sort of send-off I am after.'

I found an ally in big prop Aaron Woods, who gave me a vote of confidence on the Foxtel show *NRL 360*. 'I would love for him to be able to help the young guys coming through, give his experience to them,' Woods said. 'If I was a club boss I would definitely have a chat with him. You would need to do your research behind him first but I would want to see where he is at. I would ask him why he wants to come to the club and what he can bring.'

But it all fell on deaf ears—there were no takers, with the NRL making it pretty clear they didn't want to see me back in the big league. I didn't get it—I'd been away over three years and that was a pretty hefty punishment. I'm not bitter with them but I believe everyone screws up and everyone deserves another chance. And I can't help feeling that there isn't much consistency in the way the NRL hands down its punishments and some people seem to get off lightly while others, like me, get whacked with a big stick. Some get stood down, others are allowed to play on.

I can tell from talking to people and reading on social media that I'm not the only one who feels this way; lots of people are confused by it all. The NRL and Todd Greenberg seem to often bow to media pressure when handling these cases. When the media makes a big deal of it—which it invariably does with me—the NRL feels it has to do something to show the public that it is on top of the situation and hands out a tough punishment. I will be forever tarred as 'the bubbler bloke' in the eyes of some people, but they seem to me to be people without lives who have nothing better to do than bag me for something that happened years ago. One of my sisters reckons I should do 'the bubbler' again and make a video of it—she says I would make a fortune. She is only joking of course, but it shows the sad state of affairs in the world today that she is probably right—it would go crazy online.

So it was off to steamy Cairns I went in the summer of 2017–18 and it was a real struggle adapting to the conditions after the bitter cold of England. I hoped against hope that this would be my ticket back into the NRL, via the Pride, especially around State of Origin time when the Cowboys would likely be short on troops. I signed for two years and did plenty of work in the community, partly because I enjoy doing that stuff but also to maybe show the doubters that I had mended my ways after three years in the wilderness. I was training full-time, half the week with the Pride and then flying to Townsville to train with the Cowboys from Monday to Thursday. All the travelling wasn't ideal, and it was hard to maintain any sort of form split between two teams, but just training with the Cowboys gave me that taste of NRL and I was really hoping the cards would fall my way.

Sadly, I got news of Mum's breast cancer diagnosis mid-season and as soon as that happened I asked for a release on compassionate grounds. I didn't want her fighting the toughest battle of her life on her own. She has had a hard time of it, between Dad's illness and death and all my stunts. It was a no-brainer that I had to be closer to home to give her support. I'm so proud of her—she faced her illness with strength and dignity and has been recently declared cancer-free, which delighted the family.

I tried to keep my career alive and it looked like I got a lucky break when the North Sydney Bears showed some interest in me to play for them in the Intrust Super Premiership. Greg Florimo, their former champion centre and a great guy, was over the moon when I said I was looking for a club and happy to play for them. It was going to be win–win: I needed to be playing footy and they were looking for a 'name' player to help bring people through the gate.

We did the deal old-style—we had a coffee and I signed the back of a coaster and was a Bear, or so I thought. I got shattered again at the final hurdle, when Norths sent the paperwork to South Sydney, as they were required to do as the Rabbitohs were their feeder club. Souths' General Manager of Football Shane Richardson blew up, even threatening to cut the ties between the two teams if Norths signed me. He put it down to the fact that Souths wanted to develop their own halves when he released this statement:

We've spoken to Norths about Todd Carney and it's our position that we will develop our young halves as opposed to bringing in a player from outside the club. Players such as Adam Doueihi, Connor Tracey and Dean Hawkins are all excellent young players who we see as future players in the NRL and our efforts will be concentrated on them. We intend to [focus on] the players we have here at the club and our players, coaches and staff are all on board with this approach.

But I didn't buy it. I think Richardson didn't want a bar of 'bad boy Carney' and may have even been pressured by the NRL to have nothing to do with me. As it was, the incident created plenty of bad blood between the two clubs and the Bears switched camps to become the Roosters' feeder club in 2019.

There was a further hiccup—the Pride put a $15,000 transfer fee on my head, which annoyed me. 'He [Carney] doesn't owe us money, but we want compensation,' Northern Pride chief executive officer Greg Dowling said. 'We paid him an amount to relocate here and we want that refunded. Once they pay we'll clear him. Naturally, we were chasing a number of people and when Todd agreed, we concentrated on him thinking he would be here long-term. I've spoken to his manager and to Greg Florimo, so that's where things are at now.'

I wasn't about to pay it and neither were the Bears, but in the end it was irrelevant because of Souths' stance.

That left me down and out . . . again. My manager Dave Riolo rang English clubs again and got a positive response from Tim Sheens, who was then at Hull Kingston Rovers. I had a good relationship with Tim after our time together in the Australian team in the Four Nations championship in 2010. He is one of the most respected blokes in the game and a top coach to boot, with a string of premierships to his name, so I was thrilled that he was keen on me. Hull KR were battling relegation at the time, which can be the kiss of death for teams in the UK, and were after a quick fix. I flew out in July 2018, hoping I could help them avoid the dreaded drop to the lower league.

In my first game in twelve weeks, I tore my calf—disaster! The injury dogged me throughout my time there but I managed a few decent games and helped them stay in Super League. But the long time off the field and being so far from home made me realise England was not where I wanted to be, and I headed for home yet again—this time with my career in Super League definitely at an end.

There was some lukewarm interest from NRL clubs once again when I came back home late in 2018, especially Manly, where I feel I may have fitted in well alongside Daly

Cherry-Evans. But once more it all came to nothing, with the same old hurdle—the NRL and Todd Greenberg not keen to see me back in their competition. They were still putting roadblocks in front of me as I attempted that last-ditch return to the big league, ensuring no club would take a punt on me.

Greenberg and his men were letting other blokes who did far worse than me back into the game, but with me they would have nothing of it. The year before, they were more than happy to let Matt Lodge, a bloke who broke into a family's home in New York and terrorised them and was arrested by New York police, walk straight back into the game with the Broncos. I've got nothing against Lodge— I don't know the bloke and good luck to him for getting another crack—but he also had a bit of a rap sheet apart from that incident and, to me, the whole thing reeked of double standards. And it seems I wasn't the only one who felt that way. The respected *Sporting News* website wrote in a March 2018 editorial:

> Rugby league fans are trying to wrap their head around the fact a player who urinated in his mouth has not been welcomed back by the NRL, but one who has viciously assaulted an innocent couple and backpacker has the right to return to the game.

It has been almost four years since Todd Carney was exiled from the competition for his infamous 'Bubbler' incident which many consider a schoolyard prank.

The governing body was forced to put its foot down as Carney added yet another strike to his name after a chequered past that involved drink-driving incidents, a runner from police and alcohol bans just to name a few.

But many felt he was hard done by for his brain snap moment that went viral on the internet and forced him overseas to the Super League.

The playmaker is attempting to resurrect his career with the Northern Pride in the QLD Cup this year, but the NRL is yet to give him the green light to return to the top grade despite his clean sheet in recent years.

Yet Lodge gets a free pass?

The former Tiger will suit up in the front-row for Brisbane in 2018 just a few years after he violently attacked New York couple Ruth Fowler and Joseph Cartright, leaving his victims scarred for life.

Frightening new Channel Nine footage has emerged of Lodge putting Cartright in a headlock as he unleashed a flurry of punches before locking his victim out of his own apartment with his partner and children inside.

A US civil court ordered the Brisbane recruit to pay $US1.6 million in damages, which he has paid none of.

Despite the horrific event on his resume, NRL CEO Todd Greenberg has defended the decision to register Lodge's contract, claiming rugby league is a game of second chances.

'This young guy made a horrible mistake. He has paid a significant price for that. He's a young man and I believe rugby league is part of the solution to help him turn his life around,' Greenberg said.

'He gets a second shot but he won't get a third so what he has to do is put his head down and work really hard and demonstrate to his club and the game that this chance is everything for him and I think he will do that.

'At some point you've got to give this kid a second chance and you've got to hold him accountable to that chance. Ultimately he'll grab it with both hands or not.'

Carney's third chance is long gone, but when you put the two situations side by side, how does it make sense to look past assault and condemn urination?

So I had to accept that at 32 and after 220-odd games, my career at the elite level was over. Every player reaches that day and it's never easy—and it was tougher for me because I wasn't allowed to go out on my own terms and copped a bit of a raw deal as a result of my past sins. But I have always believed in looking ahead and not dwelling on the past. I feel I still have something to offer, as both a player and coach.

BOYD CORDNER

Boyd Cordner is one of the true golden boys of New South Wales and Australian rugby league. A cleanskin who has never been in trouble of any sort on or off the field, he has developed into a great ambassador for the code and a true leader. As with Jeff Robson, the fact that he and Todd Carney are best mates may seem a contradiction to some, but shows that Carney is perhaps not as much of a bad boy as the critics like to make out.

Cordner remembers he was in awe of Carney when the pair first crossed paths at the Roosters in 2010. 'I was this unknown, raw teenager from the bush, which is one thing we had in common,' Cordner says. 'Todd was six years older than me and an established star. I pretty much kept away from him because I thought he might brush me or something—I was only playing in the National Youth Cup. And a year earlier I was playing backyard footy with my mates then all of a sudden I was on the training paddock with superstars like Todd and Mitchell Pearce.

'Todd kept his distance too, which I later learned was because he is a pretty shy bloke by nature. Then one day, after training, I was sitting at the bus stop waiting to catch the bus home to Mascot—I'd lost my driver's licence for a while at that stage—and all of a sudden this car screeches to a halt and the window rolls down. It was Todd, who I had still barely spoken two words to at that stage—and he asked me where I was going. I told him I was heading home and he just told me to hop in. We chatted a little on the drive and when we got to my place, he said to me, "Okay, I'll be here at 8 a.m. tomorrow to take you to training." I tried to refuse—he was living in Coogee and it was way out of his way—but he insisted. And every day for the rest of the season, he'd pick me up and take me home.

'I was blown away—he was a big name NRL star and I was a nobody. But that's Todd. The public perception is so different to the reality with him. He is one of the nicest blokes I've had anything to do with in footy. His bad boy image and bravado are all as a result of a handful of bad decisions that he now regrets—all to do with the drink. He hasn't had the easiest life and I just wish the haters would cut him a little slack.'

The 'odd couple' became inseparable and would eventually become flatmates in Sydney's east, with Cordner trying—not always successfully—to keep his buddy out of trouble. 'We were flatmates for a couple of years, until he switched to Cronulla,' Cordner says. 'We found we actually had a lot in common and after we talked about our families, we worked out that we are in fact related as very distant cousins. We are both country boys who saw league as our one chance to make it big. He lost his dad early and I lost my mum, so we talked a lot about how those type of things impacted on our lives.'

Cordner knows better than anyone that the real Todd Carney is very different to the legend. 'When people found out who I was living with, a lot of them freaked out,' Cordner says. 'They said stuff like, "You need to keep away from that bloke—he is bad news!" Even my girlfriend was wary of him when she first met him and I could tell she had reservations about us being such great mates. But now as she has got to know him, she has warmed to him and realised what a great guy he is.

'There's no doubt Todd has been his own worst enemy at times and got himself in strife with some poor choices along the way in his career. But to me, he was a great mentor and his professionalism and dedication at training helped me in my development as a player. He took me under his wing— when we lived together he even did the cooking to make sure I ate healthy!'

The pair have also gone on the road together many times in their down time. 'He loves Bali and we have been there a few times—but what happens in Bali stays in Bali,' he laughs. 'One year we got stuck there because of the ash cloud from that volcano that grounded all the flights in and out. I think Todd never wanted the cloud to lift—he loves the place.

'He took me and Wade Graham back up to Atherton where he spent his year in exile and all the people up there just love him. He was so proud to take us back to the pub where he held down a "real" job and introduce us to all the locals. And we just had a laidback weekend drinking and punting—it was great.'

Cordner believes Carney has found the perfect spot to get over all the dramas of the past decade in laidback Byron Bay. 'He just loves it up there and isn't under that same media spotlight that dogged him in Sydney,' Cordner says. 'I visited him up there a while back and he was so relaxed. He said to me, "I can just be myself up here and be relaxed and low key, it's the perfect spot to chill and enjoy life," and I couldn't be happier for him—he's had a tough time of it and deserves a few breaks going his way.'

16

COACHING

I've been given an opportunity to captain–coach Byron Bay in northern New South Wales this year and I'm massively excited. It is a challenge, for sure, but I have never shied away from hard work and this is something very new and different for me. I want to be a long-term coach once my playing days are over and this is the first step on what will hopefully be a successful journey.

After all the NRL doors closed in my face, I met Ben Webber, the president of the Byron Bay club. He actually got in touch with me on Instagram, so I guess that is one of the few occasions I can thank social media for doing something good for me rather than bringing me down. I've always loved the area around the NSW North Coast so the idea of playing and living up there appealed to me. I flew up and visited Ben and his committee and they offered me the captain–coach role, which I gratefully accepted. It's a three-year deal and I'm committed to giving it my all and helping rebuild the club. Like a lot of country clubs, Byron has struggled in recent years. In fact, in 2018 the captain–coach quit mid-season for personal reasons and the club finished with the wooden spoon in the Northern Rivers Rugby League competition. So there is a fair bit of work to do, but the only way to go is up in my eyes. We have started well, the local people are right behind us and I'm a positive person and see it as a great challenge.

Byron isn't your average country town that eats and breathes rugby league. There are a lot of tourists passing through from all parts of the world who have no idea what footy is, as well as a lot of overseas people who have settled here. But there is a good, hardcore group of people who love their footy and it's been great for me to meet and get to know them. They've given me a chance and I don't plan to let them down.

I've played under some very knowledgeable coaches in my time—the likes of Matty Elliott, Tim Sheens, Peter Sharp, Shane Flanagan, Brian Smith and Neil Henry. People have asked me which one of these guys I will model myself on as a coach and I guess the answer is that I will take a little from what I have learned from each of them and be my own man—I will model myself on myself. They all had their strengths and all helped me along my road in the game. Matty was great in building relationships with players and helping them realise their potential. 'Smithy' was very technical and structured, 'Sheensy' lived and breathed the game and knew how to keep the players, board, fans and media onside—that is why he has survived for so long. He is still coaching in England after starting at Penrith in the 1980s! Neil Henry was also very structured and placed massive emphasis on discipline on the field and waiting for the opposition to make mistakes and then punishing them. 'Flanno' built a great culture at Cronulla and Peter Sharp was a top bloke who I enjoyed playing under.

It will be different in these first three years at Byron as I will be a captain–coach, hopefully leading the boys from out in the middle. I can afford to be their mate as opposed to their boss in this role and in training and pre-season, and I've been really pleased at the way they have put in. Remember, we are talking about young players with real jobs who play for a couple of hundred bucks a win and an end-of-season trip to Bali. Their lives aren't dominated by rugby league like the blokes I played alongside for many years and I have to be mindful of that.

We train twice a week and the rest of the time I don't mind if they are out surfing at the great beaches around Byron or socialising with their mates. And if a bloke can't get to training because of work, I'm not about to jump on him—this isn't the NRL up here and I get that.

I think choosing the team every week will be the hardest thing. Eighteen blokes love you but you have to keep the rest of the squad happy and motivated. I have some good people around me who will help in the selection process so it won't be just me who is making the decisions—they can't put all the blame on me!

I'm also wary that the guys will get sick of hearing just my voice week in, week out—at training, before match, at half-time and full-time—so I've got helpers who will also talk to them and give them tips. I'm happy for them to have bonding sessions, so long as things don't get out of hand, of course. I know only too well the consequences when things do spin out of control. They are young and should enjoy themselves; training or playing should never become a chore.

There are a lot of good young kids here with potential and I want to help them become the best players they can be. The next step for them, if they make the grade, is the Queensland Cup and if they do well there, maybe an NRL contract—you never know. I would be over the moon if I could help put a few of these guys onto the path to becoming full-time professionals. I see that as being a big part of my job. Having played at the elite level with and against some of the best players in the world, I would like to think I can pass on some stuff to them and help them become the best they can be. After I retire as a player, probably when my three years as captain–coach are up and I'm in my mid-thirties, I'll look at maybe getting a coaching gig in the Queensland Cup or an assistant coach role in the NRL. I'll have to change my mindset then—I will no longer be their teammate and will be more their boss and probably have to adjust the way I approach a few things. But I know I need to prove myself first and come up with the results here and my primary focus is on that. There are some wonderful people in Byron and I want to make them proud of their footy team.

Our facilities are a long way short of what the guys in the NRL have. We have no grandstand and a tiny gym to work in, but that's regional footy and it has a special charm and passion to it—it excites me. It's a new chapter, away from the pressures of the NRL, and I'm enjoying every minute of it. I have no ambitions to be an NRL head coach—I've been there as a player and the pressure and scrutiny are things I never really enjoyed. And you can multiply that times ten as a coach. I've seen what constant pressure does to guys and it's not for me—no thanks. I'd love the job of running the bottle for an NRL side—relaying messages to the players and keeping them focused and motivated. I know former champion halfback Allan Langer has done that at the Broncos for many years and I can see he loves it. It's a role that keeps you at the coalface but you can do it without waking up with every bone in your body aching the next day!

I'm also very keen to pass on my knowledge and experience to kids. I feel very strongly about giving something back to the game that gave me everything. I have seen what my good mate, sprint king Roger Fabri, has done in Sydney, helping people increase their speed and agility, and having worked with him it was something I really enjoyed. I am working on setting up my own academy for young sports people, and not just league but any game that requires pace and skill.

I've had good support up here. In Brisbane, the South Sunnybank club appointed me their development coach this year and it's only a two-hour drive from Byron Bay so I go up there a few times a week. I plan to do group training and also individual coaching for halfbacks from around under 15s to seniors, with emphasis on skills and kicking. Andrew Johns and other top halfbacks work with young NRL playmakers and maybe a role like that will come, but in the meantime I'm happy to work with young kids who have dreams—like I had.

Young people make mistakes and poor choices every day, but unless you are a 'name' you are not a media target and you just move on. I miss the NRL, but I'm also glad I'm away from it. I'm not sure I could hack being a young bloke starting their career now—the scrutiny from the public and media is greater than ever. I've spoken to old-time players who have told me that if they'd had mobile phone cameras back in the day, they probably would have ended up in jail. They realise how lucky they were and sympathise with current players and everything they have to put up with on a daily basis.

In my football career, I found I didn't go through form slumps often—only when the stuff I did off the field was hanging over my head and got to me. I imagine guys who work in banks or as salesmen are the same—if there is drama in your world, it can play with your head and affect everything you do.

I'm also looking into guest speaking—everybody seems to want to know the Todd Carney story—and getting into mentoring for young people. I can tell them what it takes to get to the top and the mistakes to avoid—certainly I've made more than my fair share so it's an area I'm pretty well credentialed in.

What would I tell a young Todd Carney now? Just to do things in moderation and think before you do something stupid, and actions have consequences; don't go crazy on the drink on a night out because it could come back to bite you. There is nothing wrong with having a good time and enjoying yourself with your mates, life is meant to be enjoyed—but if you want to be a sportsman, people will recognise you: you have to be extra careful not to do the wrong thing.

ROGER FABRI

Roger Fabri is arguably Australia's best-credentialed and highest-profile sprint coach. A former professional runner who won several Gift events, he trained alongside Olympic champions like Linford Christie and Darren Campbell and attended camps with NFL teams the New York Jets, San Diego Chargers and Dallas Cowboys in recent years. He has been named NSW Athletic League Coach of the Year a record six times and has worked with elite athletes in sports as diverse as rugby league, rugby union, soccer, AFL, cricket, ice skating and netball. Among his clients are the likes of Sonny Bill Williams, David Warner . . . and Todd Carney.

Fabri and Carney became close when the sprint guru was signed by the Roosters in 2010 as the team's official sprint coach, helping the Roosters rise from wooden spooners to grand finalists in one year.

'I remember Todd back then as this cheeky kid with raw speed and raw talent—he didn't have all the tricks he developed later in his career,' Fabri says. 'From a technical running point of view, he was messy and inefficient as a kid but developed into a beautiful mover and a graceful and natural runner with the ball in his hands. I admired him because he knew just having ability wasn't going to be enough—I think he learned that from his dad. He was always doing extra work with me and I think that improved him as a footballer because he was just so quick on his feet and league is such a speed game.

'I've worked with the best across a host of sports and I would rate him in the top three of all the people I have coached in terms of ability and athleticism—in his prime he did some freakish things on the football field. His lateral running was a thing of beauty. We also became very close on a personal level. Forget what you have read about him, he is a kind kid with a good heart.

'Of course he has made some bad decisions in life but he has been absolutely hammered for them—and kept getting up and trying again. I was angry that the bubbler prank ended his NRL career. It was a stupid thing to do but a gross over-reaction by Cronulla and the NRL.'

Fabri isn't just saying nice things about Carney to be polite—he thinks so much of the former Dally M winner that he gave him a job with his athletics academy. 'Todd has been there and done that and young students of sport always respect that,' he says. 'He is patient with the athletes and gets his message across to them well. The kids just warm to him and they listen to what he says. Not just about running but about life because he has learned some painful life lessons in his time and isn't afraid to admit it and how he stuffed up. But most of all, he is a genuine character and life around him is never dull—I can testify to that.'

17

MY TATTS

There's very little about my life that doesn't attract criticism from the wise guys out there—and that includes my tattoos. I may have gone overboard with them a bit, but they are expressions of who I am and what I believe in. They are a bit like my life itself—a bit messy and disorganised, and every time I make a rash decision in my life, it is often reflected in my next tattoo.

I got my first one when I was still a teenager in Canberra—my nanna took me to get it. It was just my name on my forearm. I regret it a bit now because it's there for life, but there are others I am happier about. When I got home with that first one, I thought Mum would flip out when she saw it. But she was fine with it and, ever since, I've been slowly but surely collecting them to the stage where there aren't too many tatt-free places on my body anymore!

Most reflect the things I believe in, such as family and enjoying life. I've got my parents' initials behind each ear and my two sisters' names printed on my wrists—they are never far from my heart. After Dad died, I got the saying 'Always in my mind, forever in my heart' tattooed on my hands so when I looked at them, I would always think of him. And I put the day he was born and the day he died on my chest. I've also got Dad's name on my neck.

On my chest are the words 'This too shall pass', just to remind me that the tough times, when you feel the whole world is against you, won't last forever. If you can ride them out, you will be stronger for it—I've had plenty of experience with that.

My left shoulder has a joker holding a bunch of playing cards with the words 'Life's a gamble', which is pretty much the way I see the world and probably sums up how I live. I've gambled—not with money but with some of my actions—throughout my life. Sometimes it has paid off . . . other times it has blown up in my face, as the pages of this book clearly show.

On my right arm are a fish and a dragon and the Latin words 'Carpe diem'. I was never much of a scholar but

I always liked that saying—it means 'seize the day' and was penned by the ancient Roman poet, Horace. Again, it's one of the things I live by. I believe you only get one shot at life so you need to make the most of it while you can.

On my arse, I have the words 'Time waits for no one', again something I strongly believe in. On one leg are the words 'Laugh now, cry later'; I guess that sums up how life can be a roller-coaster of emotions, particularly when you have experienced the highs and lows I've gone through in my 30-odd years on the planet.

Also on my legs is a saying from my own journey: 'Good times become memories, bad times become lessons'. Clearly I've had a lot of learning to do down the years. You can't turn back the clock and change the past—what's happened has happened, the good and the bad—and you just have to get on with your life and make the most of it. That's the message from that tatt.

My legs have another tattoo, of an eagle and an anchor. I'm not superstitious, but the eagle is to watch over me and the anchor is to keep me grounded, to ensure I don't get a big head and always remember where I've come from. On my side is another of my creeds, thirteen lines that read: 'Life's to [*sic*] short to wake up in the morning with regret so love the ones who treat you right and forget the ones who don't. Remember everything happens for a reason. If it changes your life. Let it. No one said it would be easy. They just promised it would be worth it to live your life and chase your dreams.'

The biggest tatt I've got is on my back—an angel with wings spread and its head in its hands. It sums up the mix of emotions and feelings you experience in life, I guess. I'm not sure where I go to from here with body art, whether I keep finding the few blank spots on my body and adding some more or give it a rest for a while. Often it is a spur-of-the-moment decision. There is one tattoo I do have planned though—the cancer symbol. Mum is getting the same one, as a statement for both of us that she had cancer and kicked its arse. She is one tough lady and I'm so proud of the way she got through that battle and want to have it somewhere on my body for all to see.

MUM

Leanne believes a good woman would complete the Todd Carney redemption story. 'When we were in France, [former Manly star] Glenn Stewart once asked Todd, "Why aren't you married?" and Todd replied, "Because I haven't found a woman like Mum." That really touched me.'

When this book went to press, Carney was dating Susie from the hit reality television show *Married at First Sight*. A single mum who lives in Brisbane, she was crazy about the former Test halfback—and the feeling was mutual. The pair took every chance to do the two-hour drive up and down the highway from Brisbane to Byron to get together in their down time and Susie had Leanne's seal of approval. 'With a nice woman behind him, he will really blossom, and Susie could be the one,' she says. 'She is nothing like they portrayed her on the TV show and I have nothing but good things to say about her—and I can tell Todd is smitten.'

Leanne—known as 'Pony' to her friends and family ('One day Daryl saw me jump out of the car and run into the shops to drop something off and said to the kids, "Look at the way Mum runs, she's like a pony," and it has stuck to this day')—has fought a brave battle against cancer since being diagnosed in late 2017. 'It was naturally a shock to us all—I guess cancer always is,' she says. 'It was in the breast and came up in a regular mammogram check-up. Todd was playing for the Northern Pride at the time, the feeder club for the Cowboys. We still held some hope that that could lead to a recall to the NRL with the Cowboys, but as soon as I told Todd, he jumped on the first plane back to Sydney. He said, "I want to be there to help you beat this thing, Mum."

'I had four months of chemotherapy, the first three were okay but the fourth was pretty rough, and then a month of radiation treatment. I have changed my diet and lifestyle—with help from Todd—and am feeling really good again. It's been an emotional battle and tough at times, but I was given the all clear earlier this year and appreciate every day even more now.

'Todd's NRL career is now over and he's thinking about life after football and made some good plans. He is actually quite smart in some of his ideas about junior coaching, setting up an academy and giving back to the game. He played at the highest level under some great coaches—he has a lot of knowledge and can also tell young players of the consequences of poor behaviour. He knows plenty about that. At Byron Bay, he went out and got sponsors for the club himself. They finished with the wooden spoon last year, and it's more a tourist town than a rugby league town, but he has already had some influence on the locals. They can see he is not the monster he has been portrayed as. He walks down the street and happily talks to anyone who comes up to him and will always pose for a photo or sign an autograph.'

THE SISTERS

The sisters know Todd better than anyone and, after all these years, put the blame for his career going off the rails squarely on the Canberra Raiders.

'He came into their system at seventeen and they just treated him as they would any other player,' Melinda says. 'What they didn't understand is that he was a teenage kid, plucked straight from home who had never had a drink, never made money and never hung out with tough, hard, fully grown men. They drank hard and partied hard and that was all new to him and clearly he didn't handle it well. He went straight from a loving home to a single room away from his loved ones at the Australian Institute of Sport in Canberra. He hated it, but the Raiders didn't care. There was no duty of care or mentoring—the club promised they would take special care of him but they never delivered on it—even after Dad died and Todd was a basket case. He had to deal with the glare of the media—they built him up and made him seem like a god when Canberra were winning and he was playing well, and then slammed him and hounded him when he played up. Again, that was all new to him and hard to handle for a kid. The media seemed to build him up and tear him down as they felt with no thought about the effect it had on him. He had no idea how to deal with it and again, the Raiders did little to help. Mum tried to talk to them and explain that he wasn't happy and needed help and guidance long before it all came to a head. They just kicked him out the door when it became all too hard for them. We are certain most of his problems would never have happened had Dad been around—but I guess we will never know.'

In the meantime, the sisters and their young children remain close to their brother and try to live a 'normal' life after all the dramas of the past. 'We are a normal family at the end of the day,' Krysten says. 'We have had our ups and downs but are always there for each other. Todd is a great brother—sometimes we laugh together, sometimes we cry together. Ironically, Todd is the quietest of the three of us. Melinda and I have been known to dance on tables at bars and think we can sing and take over the band on a night out—we have a bit of 'wild child' in us. We do stuff Todd would never dream of doing. He is far more placid and quiet. He will always listen if one of us has a problem or needs to vent and even now, we still baby him a bit because he is the youngest and fragile at times when he is under attack. He loves nothing more than playing with his nieces and nephews—Emity, Chaise, Piper, Amali and Evie. He can be strict with them but he also torments them in a loving way—just as his dad used to do with us a lifetime ago.'

18

LEGACY

How will I be remembered? I've thought about that a fair bit now my career in the big league is over. And I realise while I won the Dally M, played for New South Wales in State of Origin and for Australia, people will always associate me more with the things I'm not proud of: 'the bubbler', running from the cops, generally getting into shit on the drink. I guess I just have to live with that. I did a lot in a relatively short period of time. Some good, some bad, but at least I was never boring. I've been fortunate to have made a lot of mates through the game, guys who will be mates for life.

I played in an NRL Legends game earlier this year at Central Coast Stadium and it reminded me of how lucky I am to have played one top-grade game, let alone over 200. I spoke to one of the organisers, former Rabbitoh and Rooster Mick Crocker, and he said it was a league player's dream, hanging out with old mates, playing in a light-hearted game and reminiscing about old times—and I couldn't agree more. The legends concept is a great one and hopefully will expand in the future. I know it was well received all around. It was like a big reunion of team-mates and opponents alike. I got to mingle with guys I played with like Terry Campese and Michael Weyman, as well as legends of the game like Wendell Sailor and Willie Mason. I played for the Barbarians team—guys who weren't really aligned to any particular club—and got a late call-up because Matt King was supposed to play but he pulled out to go with the Roosters on their end-of-season trip to Los Angeles and Las Vegas after they won the premiership. Canterbury won the comp but we all bagged them—we reckon they were over the salary cap!

There was a fair crowd up there and I enjoyed mingling with the kids out the back and having a chat with them. They still remember me, which is good, and while it sounds like a cliché, I really like putting back into the game that has given me so much in life. As much as I've had bad times because of my profile as a rugby league player, I've also had some of the high points of my life and been very lucky—I owe everything to rugby league. People ask me, 'Aren't you bitter with the game and the way you were treated, being booted out for one prank too many while other guys get a slap on the wrist?' and I say 'no way'. Yes, it's been frustrating, but without footy, I hate to think where I'd be now.

The average person gets away with stuff that the Todd Carneys of the world don't. It's unfair but that's the way it is and it took me a long time to understand and accept it. If only I'd known this hard truth when I was twenty, I would have got into a lot less strife. But then that is something thousands of young men around Australia— and the world for that matter—could easily say as they look back over their lives. I just did things on the spur of the moment, it's not like I *planned* to get in trouble. The drink was my weakness and I just wish I had a filter in my head that warned me when I was going to implode. I would love to wind back the clock and change things and start my career again; I would be such a better player knowing what I do now and would have got in so much less drama, not doing the things I did down the years. 'The bubbler' would not have happened—but, to be honest, I did a lot worse things in my wild early days in Canberra. Of course it's not possible to go back in time, and I have accepted my mistakes and just tried to learn from them and move on.

I've spoken to a lot of players and they agree, while they love the game, being in the NRL is often not much fun anymore. You can't go out and just have a good time with your mates because people want to stir you up and fight you and then someone is always ready to video it . . . and before you know it, you are painted as a boofhead footballer in the media. It seems so many people are waiting for players to slip up and make mistakes and then put it out there for the world to see. I believe if you pick out 200 blokes in Australia in their twenties at random, monitor their every move over ten years, you would get all sorts of scandals and atrocities. If they suspended every bloke who did something wrong, there wouldn't be many left standing!

People often ask me if I still get in strife on the drink and I believe that I have calmed down a lot from my early days. I am in my thirties now, and no longer the kid from Goulburn facing the wide world after a sheltered childhood. I still have a drink after games and on social occasions but would like to think I have a more sensible approach to grog now.

Some league fans have always been fickle, others have stuck with me through thick and thin, and I'd like to take this opportunity to thank them for their support—it's hard to express in words just how much it has meant to me over the years. The fans are the lifeblood of the game and I try to always accommodate those who want an autograph or a photo. I'm humbled in a way that they want a piece of a quiet country lad like me.

To those people who ridicule me or have a crack at me over 'the bubbler', so be it—I'm a big boy, I can handle it. I can't change the past so there is no point dwelling on it or wondering what might have been. I'm older and wiser now and those wild days are behind me—I'm starting to settle down.

What I will say to the critics is that I worked really, really hard to get where I got. Talent alone won't get you to the top in rugby league, and I would like to think I never let my teammates or coaches down on the field.

I am very lucky to have had the career I did, setting myself up for the future while playing the sport I love, and believe the good stuff far outweighs the few crazy incidents and moments of madness. I still have to pinch myself at what I was fortunate enough to achieve.

I know the critics will say, 'You could have done more—you played one Test for Australia and you could have played twenty.' My answer to that is you can say that about just about any player and any person in life in general.

Almost everyone on the planet could have achieved more than they did and missed out on opportunities or made poor choices at times—that's just life and you can't afford to let it get you down and wonder what might have been, or it will drive you crazy. There were a lot of brilliant half-backs around in my time—Johnathan Thurston, Cooper Cronk and Mitchell Pearce, just to name a few—so to get even one cap was a blessing. Getting into trouble time and time again didn't help, I'm not denying that. Bottom line is, I consider I've been very lucky in my life. I'm in a good place, I've still got a lot of living to do and I'm looking forward to what the road ahead brings.

As well as coaching, I've got a few things I'd like to do in the future; two that come to mind are running the Gold Coast Marathon and tackling the Kokoda Track. I've got mates who have done them and they have told me they are life changing and among the best things they have experienced. I want to take some people along with me—to push us all to the limit, mentally and physically, and to get them out of their comfort zone. I feel it would help people to experience these things and it would give me a kick to assist them.

I'm not saying any of this to prove to people that I'm a good bloke. Plenty of people think I'm a dickhead and they are entitled to their opinion, but 99 per cent of them don't really know me, they just know the Todd Carney in the newspaper headlines. Everyone makes mistakes in life—admittedly I made more than most—you just have to learn from them and get on with things and make yourself a better human being. And that's good enough for me.

MY TOP TENS

The ten funniest blokes in league

You talk to old guys from bygone days of the game and they tell you there are very few characters in modern day footy—and they may be right. Things that were nothing more than good-natured pranks in the old days can land you in front of the Integrity Unit in the 2010s, but I find there are still plenty of guys with a good sense of humour. Here's my top ten funny men from my time in the game:

1. **Bryce Gibbs:** 'Gibbo' was the life of the party at Cronulla—a complete idiot who would do anything for a laugh. Had the ability to laugh at himself and

take all the jibes his teammates threw at him without taking offence—a good way to be.

2. **Mitchell Pearce:** The son of a league legend, he has had the weight of expectation on him since he was a kid. Mitch lives and breathes the game but also loves having a good time in his down time, which has occasionally landed him in trouble. Similar to me in a way, I guess—and we are best mates.

3. **Dane Tilse:** A big goofy country boy, he found both Canberra and Newcastle to be big cities! But he was very popular in both and always ready to have a laugh and a joke with his mates. On the field, a very underrated workhorse, too.

4. **Ryan O'Hara:** A very witty bloke who I played with in my early years at Canberra. Could take the piss out of any situation and relieve any tension in the camp. Like Tilse, Ryan was very underrated because he came from outside Sydney but he managed one Origin game for the Blues before moving to the UK to finish his career.

5. **Jared Waerea-Hargreaves:** No fun to play against but a barrel of laughs off the field. The big man has a big sense of humour and while he takes no prisoners once he crosses that white line, at training he is always first with a joke and a smile. A gentle giant and a softy at heart.

6. **Willie Mason:** 'Mase' is old school and some of his sledges on the field are legendary. I made my debut against him and lost sleep all week just thinking about what he would do to me—and he welcomed me to the NRL with a few choice words. We laugh about it now, when we look back, but it was anything but fun back then.

7. **Luke Lewis:** plays it with a straight bat in public but to his mates, he *is* the party. He loves doing magic tricks to amuse the team. Some are great . . . others are awful. Was a champion player for many years as well.

8. **Eric Grothe Junior:** 'Ecca' is very different from the stereotype modern footballer—he thinks outside the square and loves his music, playing in several bands. His joking nature will light up a room.

9. **James Segeyaro:** 'Chico' comes across as shy and quiet until you get to know him, but the Papua New Guinea international has a wicked sense of humour within the clubs he plays for. Loves a battle of wits with his mates and is hard to beat for a quick one-liner.

10. **Dave Taylor:** This bloke could have been anything on the field—he had the size of a giant and the skills of a halfback. A typical bush boy, he was the subject of many pranks and gee-ups, but always took them well.

The ten best playmakers I've seen or played against

1. **Andrew Johns:** I was lucky enough to play against 'Joey' a few times late in his career when I was a kid finding my way in Canberra. He was probably a touch past his best but still a brilliant all-round playmaker and the best player of our generation.

2. **Johnathan Thurston:** When it comes to competitors, no one can match 'JT'. I loved watching him throughout his career. In attack or defence, he was always so close to the ball. Never gave up until the final whistle.

3. **Darren Lockyer:** Was at the top of his game for so long and ran the Broncos attack with ruthless efficiency. A master of taking the right option and that won his team countless close games.

4. **Mitchell Pearce:** I may be a little biased here as he is a great mate but he has been a premier attacking halfback for the past decade. And he's done it with a top team, the Roosters, and a bunch of battlers at the Knights.

5. **James Maloney:** Halfbacks pride themselves on being big match players and in that department, this bloke is hard to beat. He's taken every club he has played for to grand finals and just rises to the occasion when his team needs him.

6. **Brett Kimmorley:** 'Noddy' was a similar type of player to Johns who also began his career in Newcastle. Had it all—vision, a strong running game and the ability to create tries with brilliant passes or kicks.

7. **Cooper Cronk:** One of the main reasons the Storm were so dominant over the past decade—and then won a comp with the Roosters in his first year there. Has so much time with the ball—the sign of a class player.

8. **Trent Barrett:** Big and powerful, he was a new style of five-eighth who had countless youngsters model their games on him—an indication of how dominant he was in his time. So consistent over many years.

9. **Laurie Daley:** As a young Canberra fan, 'Lozza' and Ricky were my boyhood heroes. He was both a brilliant individual player and a fine team man who was a key figure in the mighty Canberra Green Machine of the 1980s and 1990s.

10. **Ricky Stuart:** 'Sticky' combined brilliantly with Daley and had a great battle with Allan Langer for the Australian halfback spot throughout their careers. A player who would do whatever it takes to win—he hated to lose even a game of marbles.

STATISTICS

Awards and accolades

Dally M Player of the Year 2010
Dally M Five-Eighth of the Year 2010, 2013
Provan-Summons Medal 2010
RLIF Player of the Year 2010
RLIF Five-Eighth of the Year 2010

International

Test Matches—By Team

Team	Years	App	T	G	GK %	FG	Pts	W	L	D	Win %
Australia	2010	1	–	2		–	4	1	0	0	100.00%
Overall	2010	1	0	2		0	4	1	0	0	100.00%

Representative

Australia—By Team

Team	Years	App	T	G	GK %	FG	Pts	W	L	D	Win %
NSW Country	2008, 2010, 2012	3	1	4		–	12	1	1	1	33.33%
New South Wales	2012	3	–	7		–	14	1	2	0	33.33%
Overall	2008–2012	6	1	11		0	26	2	3	1	33.33%

Club Career

Australian League Matches—By Year

Team	Years	App	T	G	GK %	FG	Pts	W	L	D	Win %
Canberra	NRL 2004	4	–	–	–	–	–	2	2	0	50.00%
Canberra	NRL 2005	11	1	–	–	–	4	2	9	0	18.18%
Canberra	NRL 2006	22	12	6/6	100.00%	3	63	11	11	0	50.00%
Canberra	NRL 2007	17	12	18/25	72.00%	1	85	6	11	0	35.29%
Canberra	NRL 2008	17	4	46/67	68.66%	2	110	8	9	0	47.06%
Roosters	NRL 2010	28	16	95/119	79.83%	1	255	17	11	0	60.71%
Roosters	NRL 2011	16	6	18/26	69.23%	1	61	5	11	0	31.25%
Cronulla	NRL 2012	21	4	61/78	78.21%	3	141	10	10	1	47.62%
Cronulla	NRL 2013	21	2	45/48	93.75%	1	99	14	7	0	66.67%
Cronulla	NRL 2014	9	2	–		1	9	3	6	0	33.33%
Overall	2004–2014	166	59	289/369	78.32%	13	827	78	87	1	46.99%

Australian League Matches—By Team

Team	Years	App	T	G	GK %	FG	Pts	W	L	D	Win %
Canberra	2004–08	71	29	70/98	71.43%	6	262	29	42	0	40.85%
Roosters	2010–11	44	22	113/145	77.93%	2	316	22	22	0	50.00%
Cronulla	2012–14	51	8	106/126	84.13%	5	249	27	23	1	52.94%
Overall	2004–2014	166	59	289/369	78.32%	13	827	78	87	1	46.99%

Australian Finals Matches—By Team

Team	Years	App	T	G	GK %	FG	Pts	W	L	D	Win %
Canberra	2004–2006	1	–	–		–	–	0	1	0	0.00%
Roosters	2010	4	1	14		–	32	3	1	0	75.00%
Cronulla	2012–13	2	–	1		–	2	1	1	0	50.00%
Overall	2006–2013	7	1	15		0	34	4	3	0	57.14%

English League Career—By Year

Team	Years	App	T	G	GK %	FG	Pts	W	L	D	Win %
Catalans	Super League XX 2015	8	2	–		–	8	4	2	2	50.00%
Catalans	Super 8s—Super League 2015	4	3	–		–	12	2	2	0	50.00%
Catalans	Super League XXI 2016	18	4	4		1	25	11	7	0	61.11%
Catalans	Challenge Cup 2016	1	–	–		–	–	0	1	0	0.00%
Catalans	Super 8s—Super League 2016	2	–	–		–	–	1	1	0	50.00%
Salford	Super League XXII 2017	11	–	4		–	8	5	6	0	45.45%
Salford	Challenge Cup 2017	2	–	–		–	–	1	1	0	50.00%
Salford	Super 8s—Super League 2017	4	–	3		–	6	0	4	0	0.00%
Hull Kingston Rovers	Super League XXIII 2018	1	–	–		–	–	1	0	0	100.00%
Overall	2015–2018	51	9	11		1	59	25	24	2	49.02%

English League Career—By Team

Team	Years	App	T	G	GK %	FG	Pts	W	L	D	Win %
Catalans	2015–16	33	9	4		1	45	18	13	2	54.55%
Salford	2017	17	–	7		–	14	6	11	0	35.29%
Hull Kingston Rovers	2018	1	–	–		–	–	1	0	0	100.00%
Overall	2015–2018	51	9	11		1	59	25	24	2	49.02%

Source: www.rugbyleagueproject.org

ACKNOWLEDGEMENTS

To my dad, Daryl, who shaped me to be the man I am today, and probably the ratbag I am today, thank you.

To my mum, 'Pony', thank you for being you and thank you for being my best friend.

To my sisters, 'Blissy' and 'Jersey', thank you for your love and support and always keeping me grounded.

To my extended family, thank you for your support.

To the clubs and coaches I played for, while it wasn't always enjoyable, I appreciate your support and having me at your club.

To my teammates and opposition players, thanks for bringing out the best in me.

To rugby league in general, it was great to fulfil my lifelong dream.

To the fans, there wouldn't be a game without you.

To my closest mates, you know who you are, thanks for your support and thanks for understanding me.

To my manager, David Riolo, it's been a long journey. Thanks for sticking by my side through thick and thin.

Thanks also to my co-writer Tony Adams, without whom my story could not have been told.

A special mention to Trent Tavoletti, my finance manager and great mate. Who would have thought when we met when I was eighteen we would be in the position we are today. You have helped guide me in the right direction financially and have always been there and supported me through thick and thin. Thanks again, '9 Ball'.